WITHDRAWN

Mind Tools
for Managers

JAMES MANKTELOW
JULIAN BIRKINSHAW

100 WAYS
TO BE A
BETTER BOSS
MIND
TOOLS
FOR MANAGERS

WILEY

Published by John Wiley & Sons, Inc., Hoboken, New Jersey.
Published simultaneously in Canada

For general information about our other products and services, please contact our Customer Care Department within the United States at (800) 762-2974, outside the United States at (317) 572-3993 or fax (317) 572-4002.

Wiley publishes in a variety of print and electronic formats and by print-on-demand. Some material included with standard print versions of this book may not be included in e-books or in print-on-demand. If this book refers to media such as a CD or DVD that is not included in the version you purchased, you may download this material at http://booksupport.wiley.com. For more information about Wiley products, visit www.wiley.com.

Library of Congress Cataloging-in-Publication Data

Names: Manktelow, James, author. | Birkinshaw, Julian M., author.
Title: Mind tools for managers : 100 ways to be a better boss / James
   Manktelow, Julian Birkinshaw.
Description: Hoboken : Wiley, 2018. | Includes bibliographical references and
   index. |
Identifiers: LCCN 2017060281 (print) | LCCN 2018008034 (ebook) | ISBN
   9781119374404 (pdf) | ISBN 9781119374374 (epub) | ISBN 9781119374473
   (hardback)
Subjects: LCSH: Leadership. | Success in business. | Personnel management. |
   BISAC: BUSINESS & ECONOMICS / Management. | BUSINESS & ECONOMICS /
   Leadership. | BUSINESS & ECONOMICS / Careers / General.
Classification: LCC HD57.7 (ebook) | LCC HD57.7 .M3556 2018 (print) | DDC
   658.4/09—dc23
LC record available at https://lccn.loc.gov/2017060281

Cover Design: Wiley

Printed in the United States of America

10 9 8 7 6 5 4 3 2 1

Mind Tools is a registered trademark of Mind Tools Ltd. International Registration No. 1193379, U.S. No. 4566696, EU No. 012473377, Canada No. TMA914089, Australia No. 1608561, and New Zealand No. 993356.

This book is dedicated to Rachel Thompson Manktelow and Laura Birkinshaw for their help and support, and for their professional insights.

Contents

Acknowledgments

We would like to thank Alex Cook, Charlie Swift, Emily Watson, Geoff Drummond, Jason Byers, Jo Malone, Keith Jackson, Loran Douglas, Martin Reeves, Melanie Dowding, Natalie Benfell, Natalie McLeod, Nick Adams, Nick Payne, Ollie Craddock, Peter Longton, Rachel Salaman, Rosie Robinson, Serena Chana, Sharon Utting, Simon Nevitt, Stephen Rochester, Tim Armstrong, Tim Hart, Yolandé Conradie, and Zoe Cornish at MindTools.com for their help on different aspects of the book.

Thank you to Jeanenne Ray, Heather Brosius, Danielle Serpica, Peter Knox and Jayalakshmi Erkathil Thevarkandi at John Wiley & Sons for commissioning this book and for working with us to deliver it.

Finally, thank you to the 15,000 wonderful managers and professionals who shared their thoughts with us on what it takes to be a better boss. (Space doesn't allow us to show their names here, but you can see these online at http://mnd.tools/thankyou.)

Author Biographies

James Manktelow is founder and CEO of MindTools.com, an award-winning online learning and development company that helps tens of millions of people each year improve their management, leadership, and personal effectiveness skills.

His first career was in software development, during which time he served in a variety of development, business analysis, project management, and leadership roles, culminating with serving on the board of CQ Systems Ltd. He earned his executive MBA at London Business School in 1999 and 2000.

In 1996, his passion for excellence in the workplace led him to establish a blog he called MindTools.com, where he shared the management and personal effectiveness skills he was learning as he developed his career. By 2003, MindTools.com was receiving a million visitors per year, forming the basis of the thriving company it is today.

Mind Tools now reaches more than 20 million users each year in 160 countries, providing high-quality management, leadership, and career skills training to individual and corporate clients worldwide.

In recognition of this success, Mind Tools has won Queen's Awards for Enterprise twice – in 2012 and 2017. The company also received the prestigious Investors in People Gold standard in 2017, reflecting its commitment to developing and supporting its people.

In his time at Mind Tools, James has written, edited, or contributed to more than 1,000 articles, more than 60 workbooks, and 7 books and e-books on management and leadership, published through MindTools.com, Dorling Kindersley, and now John Wiley & Sons.

Julian Birkinshaw is professor of strategy and entrepreneurship, deputy dean for programs, and academic director of the Institute of Innovation and Entrepreneurship at the London Business School.

After a brief career in the IT world, Julian went back to school, gaining MBA and PhD degrees from the Richard Ivey School of

Business at Western University in Canada. He worked briefly at the Stockholm School of Economics before moving to London Business School in 1999, where he has been ever since. He is a fellow of the British Academy, the Academy of Social Scientists, and the Academy of International Business.

He has researched and consulted extensively in the areas of business strategy, corporate change, organization design, management, and leadership. He is the author of 14 books, including *Fast/Forward* (2017), *Becoming a Better Boss* (2013), *Reinventing Management* (2010), *Giant Steps in Management* (2007), *Inventuring: Why Big Companies Must Think Small* (2003), and *Entrepreneurship in the Global Firm* (2001), and more than 90 articles in journals such as *Harvard Business Review*. He was ranked forty-third in the 2015 "Thinkers 50" list of the top global thinkers in the field of management and is regularly quoted in international media outlets, including *CNN, BBC, The Economist, The Wall Street Journal, the Huffington Post, Bloomberg Business Week,* and *The Times.*

Introduction

I t can be hard to be a good boss.

Many of us are promoted into our first management position because we've been highly effective individual performers. But when we start to manage others, we find that the new skills we need to succeed are completely different from the ones we needed beforehand.

If we're lucky, we get a few days of management training before we start. But for many, it's straight into the deep end. There are new areas of work to get up to speed in and deadlines to meet. There are poorly performing team members who need help, and there are people to hire. With all these new calls on our time, from above and below, it's hard to know where to start.

And it isn't just when we're first promoted that we need to learn new skills. With each promotion, the work becomes more complex, the criteria for success become more subtle, and our time is increasingly spent on people-related issues. Our ability to develop and learn as an individual becomes central to our further success.

Helping People Be Better Bosses

Unfortunately, although some people learn these new management skills, many do not. For example, in the US in 2016, Gallup found that only 32% of employees were fully engaged in their work – a key measure of manager performance. And in a study by tinypulse.com, only 49% of employees were "fully satisfied" with their supervisor.

These are disconcerting statistics. No manager goes to work in the morning saying, "I'm going to make my team members' lives hell today," yet the evidence shows that there are at least as many bad bosses in the workplace as there are good bosses. Why is there such a disconnect here? We suggest there are three major factors:

The leadership mystique – We are all fascinated by the larger-than-life leaders in business and politics. Sometimes we are in awe of their ambition and their achievements; sometimes we are appalled at their narcissism. But whatever our reaction, it is these leaders who make the headlines. And this can seduce us into a view that being a leader is somehow more important than being a manager. Leaders, apparently, are the people who shake things up and make change happen, whereas managers sweep up in their wake, implementing a chosen course of action and tying up the loose ends.

This is a flawed and dangerous view. It is flawed because leadership and management aren't two distinct ways of operating; they are more like two horses pulling the same cart. Leadership is a process of social influence; management is getting work done through others. Anyone who wants to succeed in the business world needs both sets of capabilities. By privileging leadership, we allow people to take the hard work of management less seriously.

Quick-fix solutions – Glance through the shelves in a large bookstore, and you will see hundreds of business and self-help books. Although there are many different genres, a popular approach is for the author to hone in on one important skill, such as coaching, time management, or mindfulness. "Here is the hidden factor behind business success," the book title declares. "This is the one thing you need to do differently to succeed at work."

These quick-fix solutions aren't entirely wrong – the skills or attributes they focus on are always important. But they aren't the whole solution. Being effective in the workplace requires a breadth of capabilities, and it requires sufficient experience to know when to use different skills and approaches. The risk of focusing on one skill is that it gets overused and misapplied. When the only tool you have is a hammer, everything looks like a nail.

The knowing – doing gap – Despite the vast number of books that claim to unlock the secrets of success, the essence of effective management is actually no great mystery. Here is our quick summary of how to get the best out of your employees: Give them worthwhile and meaningful work to do, give them space to find their own way, provide support when it is needed, and offer recognition and praise for a job well done. These are intuitively sound pieces of advice, and there are plenty of theories and practical experience to support each one.

But even though most managers would nod in agreement when faced with this list, the behavior of many tells a different story: They often fail to convey clear messages, they micromanage, they hoard important information, and they don't offer feedback or praise. There is, in other words, a knowing – doing gap – people know, intellectually, what is required of them, but for some reason, they just don't *do* it on a day-to-day basis. Management is a somewhat unnatural act – it requires us to behave in a way that goes against our innate desire to be in control and the center of attention. And, like many other activities – golf, for example – you don't get better just by reading a book. You get better at managing by working on it and by seeking feedback and advice.

Why This Book Is Different

So what can we do to close the gap between the rhetoric and the reality of good management? This book helps you by identifying the key skills you need to be a good boss and giving you the essential information you need to start practicing them.

It is based on a body of expertise and evidence that we believe is unrivaled. Both authors have been working in the management field for more than 20 years. One of us (James) is the founder of MindTools.com, one of the most widely used sources of online advice for people in the workplace. The other (Julian) is a leading academic and writer and author of *Becoming a Better Boss* and *Reinventing Management*. And both of us practice what we preach – James as the CEO of the Mind Tools organization, Julian as deputy dean at the London Business School. Between us, we have reviewed and evaluated many thousands of tools and techniques, and we have seen how they work in a wide variety of circumstances.

And we haven't just relied on our own experience in choosing the techniques described in the book. We have tapped into the views of more than 15000 businesspeople from around the world. These people filled in a detailed survey with their views on the most important techniques in different areas. We used their ratings to help us choose the top 100 tools featured in this book. The appendix details how we did this research.

So what are the key themes in this book? What is the distinctive point of view that we offer?

First, we take a deliberately nonheroic view of the boss. Indeed, we explicitly use the word *boss* here to avoid the leader versus manager debate we talked about earlier. For us, a boss is simply someone who has people reporting to her and who is seeking to get things done by working through those people. She doesn't need charisma nor does she have to offer a grand vision. Instead, she is a pragmatic individual who understands the opportunities and constraints in her role and wants to get the best from the people working for her. She is thoughtful about the context in which she is working and adapts her style to the circumstances and to the needs of specific individuals.

To be clear, we have nothing against visionaries like Steve Jobs or Elon Musk. The world needs these one-off genius types, but they are dangerous to use as role models. You are much better off aspiring to the nonheroic approach described here because it doesn't rely on you being a genius!

Second, we avoid the quick-fix approach favored by most management books. As we have said, there are many different things good bosses do, so making the right choice involves breadth and perspective. To use a well-known analogy, we aren't giving you a hammer; we are providing the entire toolkit – a set of "mind tools." And we want you to be able to figure out when to use the hammer and when to favor the screwdriver or the staple gun.

One hundred techniques might sound like a lot, but the point here is that becoming a great boss is hard work and requires a diverse set of skills. It's also worth noting that they cluster naturally into sets of complementary techniques, and the structure of the book makes it easy to navigate through these clusters.

Third, our emphasis throughout the book is on tools – ideas that you can actually put into practice. We acknowledge the academic theories that support these tools, and we provide references for those who want to know more on the background concepts, but we focus the text on practical advice and how-to steps. As you read the book, you will find some sections that seem obvious, and this should be reassuring. Every manager is familiar with some of these techniques. The challenge is to become familiar with *all* of them so you can use the right ones at the right time.

The Structure of the Book

The boss's job is complex and multifaceted. One useful way to make sense of it is to think in terms of three concentric sets of activities (see Figure I.1).The first (in the center) is to *manage yourself* – to understand your own personal needs and capabilities, use your time wisely, cope with the challenges of the job, and develop your skills over time.

The second is to *manage your work and people*. Recall that management is getting work done through other people, not doing it all yourself, so you should be devoting most of your time and effort to the activities in this circle. It is useful to split this circle into two halves. One half is *task-focused*: This is about getting work done efficiently, solving problems, making decisions, and fostering creativity and innovation. The other half is *relationship-focused:* This involves understanding what motivates others, getting the best out of them, communicating effectively, hiring and developing people, building strong teams, and dealing with difficult situations. Obviously, most situations have task *and* relational components, so you need to learn how to blend techniques from both halves.

The third activity is to *manage your wider context*. This involves developing situational awareness – an understanding of the organization you work in and the competitive business environment in which it is operating. Then it requires you to figure out how to work effectively within that context, using honest tactics for getting ahead in your organization, making change happen, and working effectively with external stakeholders, especially customers.

Cross–Cutting Themes

Although each of these circles addresses a different set of people (yourself, your immediate team, and the rest of the organization and beyond), there are some important themes that cut across them. We would like to highlight four.

Know and Manage Yourself
- Know yourself.
- Plan and manage your time.
- Cope with change and stress.
- Manage your career.

Manage Tasks and Get Things Done
- Get tasks and projects completed effectively.
- Solve problems effectively.
- Make smart decisions.
- Foster creativity and innovation.

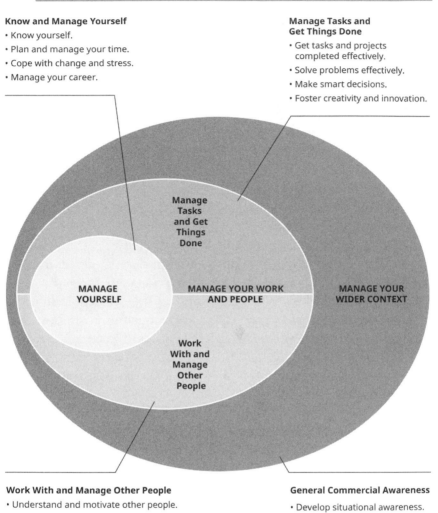

Work With and Manage Other People
- Understand and motivate other people.
- Get the best from your people.
- Communicate effectively.
- Hire and develop good people.
- Build a great team.
- Deal with difficult management situations.

General Commercial Awareness
- Develop situational awareness.
- Get ahead in the wider organization.
- Make change happen in your organization.
- Work well with customers and external stakeholders.

FIGURE I.1   Your Role as a Boss

Meaning – Research has shown that meaning, or purpose, is one of the key intrinsic motivators in the workplace. In other words, if you want to do a good job, and if you want people around you to do likewise, you need to be clear about the fundamental reason why a piece of work needs doing in the first place. For example, the best pharmaceutical firms don't just "make drugs" – they cure diseases and make people healthy.

The search for meaning cuts across many of the techniques in the book – for example, knowing yourself better, managing your career over time, getting work done in a focused way, understanding and motivating others, and making change happen in your organization.

Transparency – One of the pathologies of traditional bureaucracies is the "knowledge is power" syndrome. The boss had privileged access to information, and this helped her maintain control over lower-level employees who were often kept in the dark.

In today's business world, it is no longer possible or desirable to withhold information from frontline employees. Increased transparency helps people make better decisions, and it reduces the office politics that plague large firms. Many of the techniques in this book are about communicating more openly, encouraging people to talk more freely to each other, and building greater alignment between the top and bottom of the firm.

Simplicity – There is a tendency for large firms to build complex structures, with multiple reporting lines and large numbers of formalized procedures. In theory, these structures help them deal with complex business challenges. In practice, they often make the firm slow and unresponsive, and they make management work tedious and repetitive.

One of the themes sprinkled through the book, therefore, is the value of simplicity. The most effective bosses provide simple and clear guidelines to their employees, then they get out of the way. And the best structures are often the least encumbering ones – for example, the agile methodologies and the translation of the organization's mission into simple goals.

Perspective – Finally, and perhaps most importantly, the hallmark of a good boss is the ability to see things from different perspectives. If you can see the world through the eyes of your employees and do things that help them get the most out of their work, you will already be on the path to success. And if you have the capacity to understand how your boss, your customers, and other stakeholders see things, then you have the potential to be a great boss. It is a fascinating little paradox: The more you emphasize helping others succeed – by enabling them to do their best work – the more you will actually succeed yourself.

The bottom line is that there is no shortcut to success. This book provides the full breadth of tools you need, but you need to be prepared to work at them. So try a few of them out, then set aside time to reflect on your own behavior, find a neutral friend or colleague to bounce your ideas off of, and seek feedback on how you are doing. Then go through the cycle again – practice makes perfect. That is the real secret to becoming a great boss.

Enjoy using this book!

Part I

Know and Manage Yourself

Chapter 1

Know Yourself

L eadership is about influencing people, and a leader is someone who attracts others to follow them. So, if you want to become a more effective leader, you should start by putting yourself in the shoes of those people who work for you. What makes you worth following? Why would they want to be led by *you?*

Some leaders do this by formulating and communicating an inspiring vision to give people a sense of purpose in their work. It's great if you can do this, but the reality is that many leaders are not bold, charismatic visionaries. If you think about leaders you have worked for, some may have been like this, but others were probably quietly efficient people who got things done without a lot of fuss.

A more universal characteristic of effective leaders is that they are authentic: They bring a human touch to their work, they play to their strengths, and they are highly self-aware. To make the same point in reverse, we can all spot a boss who is faking it – someone who is trying to be the larger-than-life, charismatic leader that they have read about in business magazines. These types of people are a big turn-off, not just because they seem phony but also because they are unpredictable and hard to read, which makes our jobs more difficult. We would much prefer a boss whom we can relate to, who struggles with difficult decisions, who isn't always perfect.

This notion of authenticity is central to our current understanding of effective business leadership. It provides a good starting point for the book because it reminds us that, even though being a good boss is ultimately about understanding and enabling *others* so they

3

can do their best work, the ability to do this rests on a deep understanding of *ourselves*. Simply stated, good bosses have high levels of self-awareness, and as a result, they are able to reflect on and develop their own personal skill sets, which makes them more effective over time.

This chapter describes seven ways to help you know yourself better, to help you become more self-aware, and to help you become an authentic leader. We first describe a well-known framework for understanding your personality in the workplace (#1), then we develop two techniques for assessing your personal strengths (#2) and setting goals (#3). Next, we describe ways of improving self-confidence (#4) and self-awareness (#5). Finally, we propose two techniques for self-development – the notions of cognitive restructuring (#6) and growth mindset (#7).

1. Understand Your Own Personality and Manage Accordingly (The Big Five Personality Model)

Have you ever worked in a role that didn't suit your personality? And have you ever managed people who put in a huge amount of effort but just didn't have the right mindset for the work they did? This can be an unhappy, low performance situation for all involved, and it's why it's so important to understand your own personality – and to shape the way you manage accordingly.

One way of avoiding these situations is to be aware of and use the big five personality model, which addresses what researchers call the big five dimensions of personality:

Openness – your desire for new knowledge and experience, your appreciation of art and beauty, and your creativity.

Conscientiousness – how much care you take with things and how hard you work. This brings together factors such as industriousness, self-discipline, competence, dutifulness, orderliness, and your sense of duty.

Extraversion – how sociable you are. Are you warm, enthusiastic, and gregarious in social situations, and does being in a crowd fill you with energy? Or do you find yourself drained by social contact with new people?

Agreeableness – your friendliness and kindness to others. This includes factors such as compassion, altruism, trust, politeness, modesty, and straightforwardness.

Neuroticism – how volatile you are and how far you are in control of your emotions. It also takes into account factors such as hostility, impulsiveness, anxiety, self-consciousness, and depression.

The big five model is useful because it's actionable and because there are plenty of online tests available for it – use the second URL below to try one. So how should you use the results?

If you find that your conscientiousness is low, you need to take firm action – if you don't change this, you are not going to get far in your career because people won't be able to trust you to get things done.

Similarly, low levels of agreeableness and high levels of neuroticism are going to make you unsettling to work with, particularly in high-stress workplaces. There are strategies you can learn to manage these things (for example, see #4).

Introverts can often bring deep thinking and calm reflection to situations, but many twenty-first-century workplaces favor a faster, team-oriented, extroverted approach. Introverts need to adapt to this or find situations and roles that better suit the way they prefer to work.

Finally, greater openness is generally a good thing in the workplace. There are situations where a low level of openness may be useful: For example, we sometimes need people to make sure that rules are followed. However, if you have a low score on this dimension, you will probably want to work on trying out new experiences and ways of thinking.

Once you've used the test, think about what you have learned from it, and make appropriate plans to address these learning points.

Find out more about the big five model, and discover
strategies for addressing disadvantageous scores: http://mnd.tools/1-1
Take an online big five personality test (free):   http://mnd.tools/1-2

Source: Adapted from Judge et al. 2013. Reproduced with permission of the American Psychological Association.

2. Understand and Make Better Use of Your Personal Strengths (Personal SWOT Analysis)

We are most likely to succeed in life if we use our talents to their fullest extent and if we understand and address our weaknesses. SWOT analysis is a popular tool for looking at an organization's strengths, weaknesses, opportunities, and threats (#85). It works just as well on a personal level.

To use it, start by looking at your **strengths**. What skills, certifications, or connections do you have that other people don't have? What do you do particularly well, and what resources can you access that other people can't? What achievements are you proudest of, and what strengths contributed to these? And what do other people, particularly your boss and your coworkers, think you are uniquely good at?

Tip

If you're struggling to identify strengths, consider using the online StrengthsFinder and VIA assessments. You can access these using the URLs on the next page.

Next, look at **weaknesses**. What tasks do you struggle to do well, and why is that? What do the people around you see as your weaknesses? Where are they likely to think you need more education or training? What poor work habits do you have, and what weaknesses do these point to? What areas of development have been highlighted in past performance reviews? And what internal factors do you think are holding you back from being fully successful at work?

Then, explore **opportunities**. Brainstorm emerging trends that excite you in your market or things that customers complain about that you can address. And identify opportunities that come from your strengths.

Finally, look at the **threats** you face. What could undermine you or cause problems at work? Is your job or technology changing in a way that could be worrisome? And could any of your weaknesses lead to threats?

By this stage, you'll likely have long lists in each of these categories, and this can make your analysis unfocused and difficult to use. Prioritize these lists, and then cut them down so that they show the top three to five strengths, weaknesses, opportunities, and threats – these are the ones you should focus on. We'll look at how you can start to act on these things next.

Find out more about personal SWOT analysis, including a SWOT analysis template:	http://mnd.tools/2-1
Take the StrengthsFinder assessment ($):	http://mnd.tools/2-2
Take the VIA character strengths assessment (free):	http://mnd.tools/2-3

3. Set Clear Personal Goals, and Show a Strong Sense of Direction (Personal Goal Setting)

Just as you need to understand your own personality and your strengths and weaknesses, it is important to have a clear idea of where you want to go with your life and what you want to achieve.

Personal goal setting is a popular and well-validated approach for thinking about your ideal future and for creating the plans that will bring it to fruition. It's used by businesspeople, athletes, and high achievers to give themselves the focus and motivation to succeed at the highest level.

Setting personal goals takes only a few hours. These can be some of the most valuable hours of your life!

Start by thinking about what you would love to be doing in 10 years' time, and write down your dreams of what your ideal future will look like then. Think about the obvious areas such as personal meaning, career, family, and athletic achievement, as well as areas such as education, relationships, personal finances, personal enjoyment, and so on. You'll end up with a very long list, so choose three to five dreams that excite you most and that best suit your personality and your strengths.

Now turn these dreams into hard goals. Write them as specific statements of what you want to achieve. This is where the

SMART mnemonic is useful: Your goals should be specific, measurable, achievable, relevant, and time-bound. They should also be stretching – difficult but achievable – and emotionally engaging. Review them, and decide whether you need to prioritize further so you can achieve the ones that matter most.

The next stage is to take these 10-year goals and break them down into shorter subgoals – 5-year, 1-year, 1-month – that you'll need to achieve along the way. This takes a lot of self-discipline, but you'll be in a more focused position once you've done it.

Finally, add your goals to your action program (see #10). This gives you the framework to bring them to life by working toward them every single day.

Find out more about personal goal setting, including
accessing a structured goal setting program ($):   http://mnd.tools/3-1
Learn more about SMART goal setting: http://mnd.tools/3-2

4. Build Your Self-Confidence

Just as we want the people we rely on to be focused, we also want them to be quietly self-confident. Who would want to be operated on by a nervous surgeon, flown by an anxious-looking airline pilot, or managed by a flustered boss who doubts his or her own judgment? But how do we, as managers, develop and project this self-confidence ourselves – and in an authentic way?

There are two key concepts that contribute to self-confidence: *self-efficacy* and *self-esteem*. Self-efficacy is related to a specific type of work, and it's the self-confidence that comes from doing it well. Self-esteem is the more general notion that we can cope with what's going on in our lives and that we have a right to be successful and happy. If we have good levels of self-efficacy and self-esteem, we tend to show initiative, we're motivated, and we persist in the face of resistance.

The way we view our own abilities is a key determinant of self-efficacy and self-esteem. We can pump ourselves up with positive self-talk and listen to people who flatter us, but this can lead us to become overconfident and to fall flat on our faces. Alternatively, we can put ourselves down and listen to naysayers and critics, leading us to back away from opportunities and not achieve our potential.

So how do you get a healthy balance between these two extremes? Research has shown that being *slightly* overconfident in your own abilities is useful because it allows you to take on challenges from which you can learn. Here are some practical steps to follow:

- ◆ Understand your own personality, and plan to make the best use of your strengths, as described in #1 and #2.
- ◆ Set clear goals for the future, as discussed in #3. This gives you a strong sense of direction and highlights the areas where you want to develop self-efficacy.
- ◆ Reflect on your education and your work history so far, and list your successes and achievements in these areas.
- ◆ Now, map out the knowledge, skills, and connections you'll need to achieve your goals.
- ◆ Set small, incremental objectives to build toward your long-term goals. Focus on accomplishing these, and reflect on the skills you have developed along the way.
- ◆ Then, little by little, take on more challenging tasks or activities. If you fail at something, treat it as a learning experience. Take time to understand why you failed, and adjust your course or try again.
- ◆ As you feel your self-confidence building, make your goals bigger and the challenges tougher. And expand the skills you've learned into related arenas.

If you do all of this, and keep reflecting on what you've achieved, you'll find your self-confidence growing in a robust way. There is no need to be boastful or grandiose – you can be confident in where you are and what you've done, and that's all that you'll need.

Tip

Sometimes people work hard and achieve incredible things but still feel unworthy of recognition. If this describes you, read our impostor syndrome article at the URL on the next page.

Find out more about building self-confidence: http://mnd.tools/4-1
Learn how to combat impostor syndrome: http://mnd.tools/4-2

5. Be Aware of How Your Actions Impact Others (Journaling for Self-Development)

In addition to self-confidence, self-awareness is one of the things people most look for in their managers. Self-aware managers are good at seeing things from the perspective of others – they understand how their actions affect the people around them, and they can adjust their behavior in a way that makes them effective and generally well-regarded.

Although people differ in their natural levels of self-awareness, everyone can improve in this important area, and the most effective way of doing this is by journaling.

Journaling involves making a record of your thoughts, feelings, and experiences on a regular basis. Many people use a notebook, but other formats – video or audio journals or smartphone apps – can also be effective.

Journaling can sound like a lot of work, another thing to fit into a hyperbusy schedule. But it doesn't take much time, and it's one of the most effective ways of improving your self-awareness and growing, professionally and personally, as a result.

Start in a small way, perhaps spending just 10 minutes reflecting on your day during your commute home. Make notes on what happened, focusing on your interactions with other people and what you could have done to make them more successful. Ask yourself questions such as:

◆ What have you learned since your last entry?
◆ What difficult or painful events have occurred, and how could you have handled them better?
◆ What progress have you made toward your goals, and how could you make even better progress?
◆ What are three to five good things that happened in your day? (Finishing on a positive note is important: If it's hard to think of positive things, count your blessings and remind yourself of the people you love or the things that are good in your life.)

Tip

When you journal, take care to not dwell on negative emotions – this can be depressing and demotivating. Instead, reflect actively and learn from interactions.

You'll get a lot of value from journaling in the first couple of weeks. You may find you get diminishing returns on your effort, so continue only if it's useful. It may be something you return to when you're experiencing changes or difficulties at work or when you're not achieving personal goals as quickly as you'd like.

Find out more about journaling for professional development: http://mnd.tools/5

6. Think Positively and Manage Negative Thoughts (Cognitive Restructuring)

Can you recall a situation when a boss came into work in a bad mood? Perhaps he had been worrying about problems overnight, or she had had a bad commute. He or she probably came in looking cold or cross, maybe snapped at people, and spread unhappiness and anxiety throughout the team, reducing people's performance.

Just as we need to be appropriately self-confident as managers, we also need to be aware of and manage the emotions we project to members of our teams. From the moment we come in the door in the morning to the time we leave, people read our words and our body language. For our teams to be happy and productive, we need to project positive emotions. More than this, we need to be positive for our *own* good at work.

So, how can we think and behave positively, even when things aren't going well? As a first step, force a smile onto your face for several minutes before you enter the office. Because of the way our brains are "wired," this genuinely helps you relax and makes you feel better. (Try it; this works.)

But we also need to understand and turn around the negative thinking that underpins our own negative emotions. Cognitive restructuring is one thoughtful way of doing this. It draws from the broader field of cognitive therapy, and it offers a step-by-step process:

1. **Calm yourself.** Use deep breathing to relax yourself and deal with the immediate upset you're experiencing.

2. **Describe the situation.** Write down a precise description of the situation that has upset you.

3. **Write down the emotion** this has caused. For example, are you anxious, sad, angry, or embarrassed?

4. **Write down the automatic thoughts** that came into your mind when you felt the emotion. These might be things such as "he doesn't respect me" or "maybe I'm not good enough at this job."

5. **Write down the evidence that supports** these automatic thoughts. This may be upsetting, but you may find that there isn't much evidence that supports them. (Writing this down helps you clear your mind and take a more objective approach to the questions that follow.)

6. Next, look for and **write down the evidence that contradicts** these thoughts, and describe any alternative explanations for what has happened. If you're working hard and doing your best, you may find a lot of these.

7. Now, **write down what you think the real situation is and what action you need to take.** Depending on what you conclude, you may need to take action – for example, by apologizing to someone, seeking out coaching in an area you're struggling with, or giving appropriate feedback to people with a view to them changing their behavior.

8. Finally, **reflect on your emotions**. How do you feel about the situation now? It's likely that you'll feel much better about it.

Although this process seems quite involved, you can go though it quite quickly, and it gives you a practical way of dealing with negative thinking.

> ## Tip
>
> We've already highlighted that leaders need to be authentic – it's important to understand and be true to your personality, your strengths, and your values. However, this does not fully extend to the emotions you project to others. You are responsible for the morale of your team, and managing your own emotions is a core part of the emotional intelligence (#53) you need to lead people effectively.

Find out more about cognitive restructuring:	http://mnd.tools/6-1
Learn more about other aspects of emotional intelligence:	http://mnd.tools/6-2

Source: Adapted from Greenberger and Padesky 2016. Reproduced with permission of Christine A. Padesky.

7. Adopt a Self–Development Mindset (Dweck's Fixed and Growth Mindsets)

Linked to self-awareness is an understanding of how people grow and develop. An important concept here is Stanford psychologist Carol Dweck's notion of fixed and growth mindsets.

People with a fixed mindset believe intuitively that they have a fixed amount of intelligence, talent, and ability and that this doesn't change over time. They worry that some things are beyond their capabilities, they fear that they'll be "found out" and surpassed (perhaps by highly skilled subordinates), and they may prefer to avoid doing difficult or novel tasks rather than risk the shame of failing at them.

By contrast, people with a growth mindset believe that someone's full potential is unknowable. Where they are now in terms of intelligence and ability is the starting point for where they could be in the future, particularly if they work hard and take on difficult and interesting challenges. Failure is no big thing; setbacks are just a prompt to learn more and to try again in different ways.

Clearly, it's much better to have a growth mindset than a fixed mindset, and it's more likely to lead to a whole range of positive outcomes in your teams. However, when you look honestly into yourself, you may be surprised to find that you have much more of a fixed mindset than a growth mindset. How can you change this? Dweck suggests the following steps:

1. **Listen to yourself.** What's going on in your mind when you're thinking about taking on a new project? Do you find yourself questioning whether you have the skills or talent for it or worrying that people may look down on you if you fail? If you do, challenge these beliefs rationally, perhaps using the cognitive restructuring approach we looked at in #6.

2. **Recognize that you have a choice.** Everyone faces challenges and setbacks through life, but the way you respond makes a huge difference. Force yourself to identify opportunities to take a different path from the one you would normally take.

3. **Challenge your fixed mindset.** When you hear yourself thinking from a fixed mindset perspective, remember that you *can* learn the skills you need to achieve your goals. For example, if you're facing a challenge and you think, "I don't think I'm smart enough to do this," then challenge yourself with "I'm not sure if I can get this right the first time, but with practice and determination, I can learn."

4. **Act.** When you work on developing a growth mindset, it becomes easier to tackle obstacles in a more positive way. Think of it like practicing the guitar: It takes time, and nobody plays perfectly the first time. When you make a mistake, try to see it as a chance to learn and grow.

And how can you do this for your team? Make sure that you build an open, trusting environment where people feel comfortable expressing their concerns and their doubts. Talk about fixed and growth mindsets, and praise hard work and determined effort, even if it doesn't meet with success. (Dweck's advice is to praise effort rather than success; however, we need both in business.)

Tip

Generally, it's a good thing to encourage a growth mindset and to treat short-term failure as a "learning experience." However, a risk-averse mindset is often appropriate in high-risk situations, such as where people's health or safety are at stake, where regulatory compliance is needed, or where large sums of money are involved. In these situations, be nuanced in the way you apply this idea.

Learn more about Dweck's mindsets: http://mnd.tools/7

Source: Adapted from Dweck 2007. Reproduced with permission of Pearson Education, Inc.

Other Techniques for Knowing Yourself

The tools we've highlighted here were rated as the most important techniques of their type by the participants in our survey. You can view five other good tools that didn't "make the cut" at http://mnd .tools/c1c.

Chapter 2

Plan and Manage Your Time

H ere is a simple and important question to consider: What is your scarcest resource during the work day?

Most people have a ready answer: My time! Sure, time is a scarce resource for everyone, and most of us feel we don't have enough of it. But this is actually the wrong answer. Consider your close colleagues in the workplace. Most of them work for a similar amount of time every day, yet some are dramatically more productive than others. And these differences aren't just about expertise – the smartest or most competent person isn't always the most efficient one.

So what is the scarcest resource? It is your attention – your capacity to focus on the right things at the right time. This has always been true to some degree, but it is becoming even more important. In a world where information is plentiful, where the costs of searching for the information you need is almost zero, the premium on attention and focus is even higher than it used to be.

Simply put, the most productive and efficient managers are the ones who understand and manage their attention properly. They are sufficiently self-aware to know when they are doing valuable work and when they are wasting time, and they have the self-discipline to switch their attention toward the places where it is most valuable.

In this chapter, we describe a series of techniques and tools that help you manage your own personal time at work. The first, activity logs (#8), is simply about tracking what you are spending time on so that you know yourself better. Then we describe how to prioritize tasks effectively in terms of the amount of effort needed and the impact achieved (#9). We then describe two techniques for monitoring and tracking work – action programs (#10) are a good way of keeping major tasks and specific actions linked together nicely, whereas task scheduling (#11) is useful for planning the days and weeks ahead to make time for the most important work.

Finally, we tackle the psychological dimensions of being effective in the workplace. First, we consider the concept of flow, the state of being where people do their best work (#12), and then we address the problem of procrastination in terms of when it happens and what we can do about it (#13).

8. Find More Time in Your Day by Eliminating Low-Yield Activities (Activity Logs)

In the previous chapter, we looked at how important it is to set personal and career goals to give yourself the focus to succeed (#3). So how much of your time do you spend doing things that don't contribute to your work objectives or your personal success?

Memory is a poor guide because we tend to have a better recollection of the more valuable activities we undertake and we forget about the time spent on low-value activities. This is where activity logs are useful.

To keep an activity log, download our template using the URL on the next page, or set up a new spreadsheet with column headings for Date, Time, Activity Description, Duration, Goal/Objective Contribution (0–10) and How I Feel (0–10).

Without changing the way you work, record everything you do. Every time you switch to a new activity, whether working on a document, answering e-mails, visiting online news sites, talking to someone on instant messaging, making a cup of coffee, or chatting with colleagues, make a note. Record the time spent on the activity, score how much it contributed to your objectives, and score how focused and alert you felt at the time.

Yes, this is painstaking work. One way to encourage yourself to follow through is to agree with a peer or your boss that you are going to do it and share the outcomes with them.

After a couple of weeks, review your activity log. You may be shocked by how much time you spend on activities that contribute little to your objectives! You may also spot times of the day where you're sharp and effective, and others where you feel flat or tired.

Once you have this data, take the following actions:

1. Eliminate, delegate, or automate activities that contribute little to your goals and objectives. Be ruthless with your e-mail and IM. And sorry, the news sites and social media at work have got to go!

2. Change your work patterns so that you do your most important activities when you are most alert. Save more routine, lower-value work for the times when your energy is lowest.

3. Avoid multitasking, and minimize the number of times you switch between activities. Multitasking is inefficient, and it reduces the quality of the work you do. It is also good practice to answer e-mails in a focused way, say for one hour per day, rather than intermittently throughout the day.

4. Keep an eye out for a pattern of doing easy, low-value tasks when you should be doing important work. Procrastination is a career killer – we look at how you can deal with it in #13.

By doing these simple things, you'll achieve a whole lot more with your time and your life. If you're under pressure, keeping an activity log is the first thing to do to fix this!

Tip

Don't completely cut casual relationship-building activities out of your day – it's important to have good relationships at work. Just be focused with the time you spend catching up with other people.

Find out more about keeping an activity log, and download our template: http://mnd.tools/8

9. Prioritize Tasks Effectively for Yourself and Your Team (Action Priority Matrix)

Once you've cut the lowest-yield activities out of your day, the next stage is to focus on the activities that create the biggest impact for you and your team. This is the art of prioritization, and it's one of the most important skills you can learn to be effective at work. There are many ways you can prioritize, and you need to use your judgment to choose between them. These include prioritization based on:

♦ The objectives and key results (#27) set for you by your boss and your organization. This addresses the big picture of aligning your work with organizational objectives.

♦ Your career and personal goals (#3). Yes, you need to do the things your organization asks you to do, but you should also prioritize actions that help you achieve your career and personal goals. (We look at how you can do this in #10.)

♦ Work that unlocks the success of other people. Sometimes a small amount of work from you allows others to achieve important results.

♦ The value and profitability of potential projects that you're looking at. This helps you maximize your business impact.

One of the most useful approaches to help you choose between projects is an action priority matrix, an approach to prioritization that has been in general use for several decades. It asks you to plot each project you're considering on a grid like Figure 2.1.

The horizontal axis shows the effort needed to complete a task, and the vertical axis shows its potential impact, for example, in terms of profitability. The grid is split into these quadrants:

Fill-ins: These tasks are quick and easy to do; they give you a warm "buzz" of satisfaction when you complete them, but they don't achieve much. Some can be done quickly and painlessly; others should be delegated or dropped.

Thankless Tasks: These are big projects that soak up a lot of time but yield little return. It should be possible to cancel or reposition some of these projects; others may be suitable for delegation to a junior colleague.

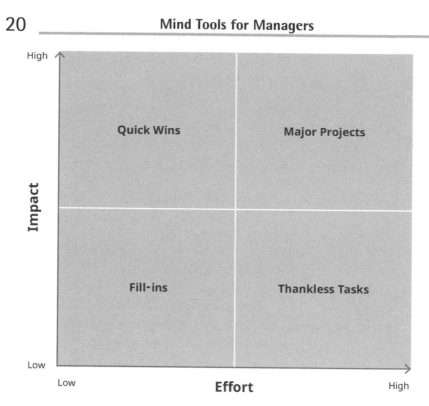

FIGURE 2.1   **The Action Priority Matrix**

Quick Wins: These are great projects that give you a high return for relatively little effort. It is usually smart to prioritize these tasks.

Major Projects: These are the most challenging tasks in terms of prioritization, as one major project like this can crowd out many quick wins. Engage with these in a cautious and disciplined way, and work on them alongside your quick-win tasks.

Tip

Effort is relatively easy to assess, but impact is often highly subjective. Make your best guess here. Also, don't put too much weight on where boundary lines lie on your action priority matrix: There may be only a tiny difference in impact and effort between something classified as a quick win or a thankless task. Good judgment is important here!

Find out more about prioritization:	http://mnd.tools/9-1
Find out more about action priority matrices, and download our template:	http://mnd.tools/9-2

10. Use a Structured Approach for Tracking and Prioritizing Many Tasks (Action Programs)

As managers, we typically have a full workload with many day-to-day tasks. On top of these, we have the career and personal goals we want to work toward (#3) and the objectives our organizations want us to achieve (#27).

It's all very well knowing how to prioritize, but how can we bring many tasks together in a coherent way without getting swamped by the sheer volume of things that we need to do? (To-do lists work well when you have a small number of things to do, but they often become too long to be practical.)

This is where action programs are useful. In essence, they are two-part to-do lists, made up of a project catalog and a next-action list.

To set up your action program, create a new spreadsheet or word processor document on your computer, or use apps like Nozbe or Remember the Milk.

Start with your project catalog. This is a detailed inventory of all the things you need to do, and you use it to make sure you don't forget anything. It can run across many pages, and it lists *everything*—routine actions that you need to perform, personal and career goals that you want to accomplish (which you should now treat as high-priority projects), objectives and key results that you've set, and one-off tasks that you need to complete.

Group related items into clusters, and tidy your list so that tasks appear only once. Low-value activities and thankless tasks should be deleted. (You can also prioritize projects (#9) at this stage.)

It takes a couple of hours to do this thoroughly, but you'll only have to do this once. You are left with a clear view of everything you need or want to do, which you can add to on an ongoing basis. Even better, you'll ditch forever the sense of anxiety and panic that comes from worrying that you've missed or forgotten something important.

Now create your next-action list. This is one page long, and it goes in front of your project catalog. It functions as a traditional to-do list, focusing on the specific actions you're going to take over the next few days to deliver the most important things in your project catalog.

To create this list, go through your project catalog, identify the highest-priority projects (making sure that these combine goal- and objective-related actions, as well as urgent routine tasks), and list the 10 to 20 logical next actions needed to move these projects forward.

Your action program is now your personal control center. Focus on completing the tasks on your next-action list. Then go back to your project catalog and bring forward the next group of specific tasks. Providing that you're disciplined and you bring forward the right mix of actions each time, you'll soon find yourself making robust, well-controlled progress toward your goals and objectives.

Tip

Action programs are powerful and you can do a lot more with them, including managing tasks that you've delegated. For more on them, including seeing worked examples, use the URL below.

Find out more about action programs: http://mnd.tools/10

---

11. Schedule Your Time Effectively

Action programs help you identify the most important tasks, but how do you make time to work on them during a hyperbusy working week?

This is where scheduling your time effectively becomes key. You have to be honest about what you can realistically achieve in a given period of time so that you create time for the things you need or want to do and you turn away low-priority activities ("Sorry, but my schedule is full until the 27th").

Set a regular time to plan your schedule – for example, at the end of each week preparing for the week ahead. Go through the following steps:

1. Identify the time that you want to make available for work, and block out the time that you won't be available, so no one can book appointments in it. (If you're ambitious, you may choose to work beyond contractual hours. But do this in a controlled way to make time for other important things in your life.)
2. Plan in the high-priority tasks from your action program (#10). Schedule these for the times of day when you're sharpest and most alert (see #8).
3. Add the essential actions needed to do your job effectively. For example, if you manage people, schedule team meetings and one-on-ones.
4. Now add in contingency time for urgent and unplanned tasks – such as dealing with customer issues – that come up in any working day. You should have a feel for how much of this you need – and be realistic, or you'll be working later than you want almost every day.
5. The space that's left in your schedule (if there is any) is "discretionary time" that you can use for other tasks on your action program.

By the time you get to step 5, your schedule may be full or even overloaded. This is where you need to go back through it and prune out the least important activities.

This involves making difficult choices, and you may need to tell people you can't deliver projects until after they want them. However, by having a well-planned schedule you have evidence that you're managing your time effectively and that you're doing everything you sensibly can to deliver these projects on time.

A well-planned schedule also gives you a great basis for negotiating sensible delivery dates for work, and it helps you build a reputation for reliability.

To be clear, this type of scheduling is painstaking and requires a high level of self-discipline to follow through. You may find it useful to work with a colleague on this process to affirm your commitment to the changes you need to make.

Find out more about scheduling, including learning how to
do even more with your time: http://mnd.tools/11

---

12. Keep Yourself Focused: Managing Distractions, Improving Flow

We've looked at how you can organize yourself to make the best use of your time. Now, we look at how you can work better, starting with developing the intense state of concentration known as *flow*, where people do their best work.

Flow occurs when all your conscious thought is focused on what you are doing. Although it has always existed as a state of mind, it was first described in detail by psychologist Mihaly Csikszentmihalyi, who said that flow involves "being completely involved in an activity for its own sake. The ego falls away. Time flies. Every action, movement, and thought follows inevitably from the previous one, like playing jazz. Your whole being is involved, and you're using your skills to the utmost."

So, how can we achieve this state of flow?

Partly it's about doing work we care about and enjoy, and that is challenging but not quite beyond our abilities. If you've used the tools in Chapter 1, you'll hopefully be on your way toward this.

It's also about managing pressure so that we're in the "sweet spot" where we're sufficiently motivated to do a good job but not under so much pressure that we get flustered (we'll look at this more in #17).

However, we also need to manage distractions and interruptions so that we can concentrate effectively. To do this:

◆ Arrange your workspace so that you're in a quiet area, and consider putting on headphones so that people know they shouldn't distract you. (You can play white noise or music to block out the hustle and bustle around you.)

- Switch off your phone and social media, and disable e-mail alerts, instant messaging, and other notifications.
- Think positively. Silence distracting negative thoughts using the cognitive restructuring approach we looked at in #6. This helps you move into the open, exploratory mindset you need to be creative.
- Don't multitask. There's no way you can devote your whole attention to one task if you're trying to do other things at the same time.
- Keep a log of common interruptions and distractions, and later, take intelligent action to minimize these. Sure, it may take some weeks to sort out everything that's distracting you, but before you know it, you'll be getting the uninterrupted time you need to do your best work.

Reducing distractions is a good way of improving focus, but that doesn't mean you will always reach the nirvana-like state of flow described by Csikszentmihalyi. The broader question of how you shape your career so that you do work you find intrinsically interesting and fulfilling is one we address in Chapter 4.

Use the URLs below to learn more about how to focus and get into flow.

Learn more about managing distractions:	http://mnd.tools/12-1
Find out how to manage interruptions, including downloading our interrupters log template:	http://mnd.tools/12-2
Learn more about the state of flow and how to get into it:	http://mnd.tools/12-3

13. Beat Procrastination

Beating procrastination is another important ingredient of effectiveness at work. We are all prone to some level of procrastination, but for 20% to 25% of people, it's a problem that seriously undermines their ability to do their jobs.

Procrastination occurs when someone *voluntarily* delays important work they know they need to complete. They know this is irrational, they're anxious about doing it, and they know it's going to cause problems, but they do it anyway. The result is that they fail to achieve objectives on time, they are seen as flaky and unreliable, and their career prospects are damaged.

So why do people procrastinate? It's something that can be associated with perfectionism, low self-esteem, and fear of failure – we look at how you can address these in Chapters 1 and 3. It can be linked to having to do difficult or unsatisfying work we don't believe in. It can be caused by low conscientiousness and a lack of self-discipline. And it can be linked to a belief that "I work better under pressure." (If a job is boring, that can be true; however, when you leave a job for the last minute, you're increasing the risk that you won't finish on time and that you'll let people down.)

Whatever the cause, you've got to get on top of procrastination and control it.

Start by recognizing whether you are prone to procrastination. For example, do you often find yourself doing small, low-value tasks rather than tackling big, difficult jobs? Do important jobs get stuck on your to-do list or action program for a long time without you doing anything about them? Do you wait for the "right mood" or "right time" to tackle important tasks? And do you find yourself leaving work until the last minute and sometimes missing deadlines? (If you have any doubts, use the URL below to take our "Are You a Procrastinator?" self-test.)

If you do find yourself procrastinating, you need to understand *why* you're doing it. For example, perhaps you find certain jobs boring or unpleasant, and, deep down, you're trying to avoid them. You may feel overwhelmed by them and seek comfort by doing small, easy tasks instead. You may be disorganized with no clear idea of priorities and deadlines. Or you may be prone to perfectionism, and you may subconsciously think, "I don't have the time and resources to do a great job, so I won't do it at all."

Whatever your reason, procrastination is a habit that you need to break. Some of the strategies below may be useful:

◆ Set well-defined goals (#3), have a clear understanding of the work you need to do (#10), prioritize tasks (#9), and plan when you're going to complete them (#11). This will help you understand the urgency of the work you're doing.

◆ Break large projects down into smaller tasks of one or two hours' duration. Get started on one of these, even if it isn't necessarily the most logical one to begin with.

◆ Give yourself small rewards – a cup of gourmet coffee or a quick walk in the spring sunshine – when you've completed a difficult task.

◆ Use the Pomodoro technique of working flat out on unpleasant tasks for timed sprints of 25 minutes interspersed with short 5-minute breaks doing something different that you enjoy.

◆ Discipline yourself to do the day's most unpleasant task first thing in the morning. Not only will you do it when you're freshest and most self-disciplined, but after that, everything will get better!

◆ Work out the cost of your time to your employer and the importance of your task to your customer. Shame yourself with this if you're tempted to loaf. And remind yourself of the negative consequences if you don't finish on time.

◆ Get people to check up on your progress. You won't want to look bad in front of them!

You'll find more strategies that address other causes of procrastination using the URLs below. Procrastination is a career killer – if you're a procrastinator, you need to do something about it!

Take our "Are You a Procrastinator?" self-test:	http://mnd.tools/13-1
Find out more about the Pomodoro technique:	http://mnd.tools/13-2
Discover more strategies for dealing with procrastination:	http://mnd.tools/13-3

Other Techniques for Planning and Managing Your Time

There are plenty of other good planning and time management techniques that didn't make the cut in our survey. Go to http://mnd.tools/c2c to find out more about them.

Chapter 3

Cope with Change and Stress

We live in a fast-changing world. As leaders of other people, we need to keep up to date with new technologies and social trends, but we also have to be prepared to adapt, on the fly, when sudden problems or opportunities arise. Recall the famous quote by Rudyard Kipling: "If you can keep your head when all about you are losing theirs and blaming it on you ... you'll be a Man, my son."

How you cope with setbacks is one of the defining qualities of being an effective boss. Yet it isn't immediately obvious, when times are good, which individuals have the "right stuff" and which do not. Warren Buffett said that it's only when the tide goes out that you see who is swimming naked. His point was that all fund managers can make money in a bull market, but when the market turns down, you figure out which fund managers actually know what they are doing and which ones don't. And it's the same in the world of management. Most bosses appear competent when the company is doing well, but when a crisis or downturn hits, you get to see which bosses know what they're doing – and which ones are swimming naked.

As with all important attributes, some people seem to have an innate ability to respond in the right way when crisis strikes so that problems are averted and those around them feel reassured. But in reality, coping with change and stress is not something you are intrinsically born with. It is a skill that you develop over time, and

28

it's an area where the true experts are the ones who have taken the trouble to learn from their experiences.

So, this chapter is all about how to develop the personal qualities and skills you need to manage adversity – how you stay on top of things, how you cope with your own concerns, and how you set the right tone for others. If we had to choose a single word to sum up the qualities you need in this volatile business world, it is *resiliency* – the capacity to respond quickly, or bounce back, when faced with adversity. The first part of the chapter explains how to increase your personal resiliency (#14). Then we describe a couple of specific tools for analyzing and eliminating stress (#15) and for managing negative emotions including anger (#16). We move on to examine the right level of pressure to produce optimum performance (#17) and look at how to overcome fears of failure or success (#18). Finally, we describe a general tool for learning from experience, Gibbs's reflective cycle (#19).

14. Develop Personal Resiliency, and Grow from Setbacks

We have all experienced tough times at work. Pressure can be intense, people get emotional, and sometimes things go wrong.

The way leaders react in these situations is important. If they react in a calm, clear-thinking way, they can bring their people together to work effectively and "weather the storm." If they dither, lose focus, or get overwhelmed, the organization will react ineffectively, and serious problems can follow.

This is why resiliency is so important. Resiliency is the ability to bounce back and achieve positive outcomes in the face of adversity. It's a capability we need to develop as leaders so that we can offer the support and direction people need when times are hard.

Personal resiliency comes from a combination of clear goals, positive attitudes, well-developed skills and experience, self-confidence, and strong support from those around you. Resiliency comes from within, but it can be enhanced by working in a supportive environment where trust and teamwork flourish.

The good news is that if you've mastered the skills in Chapter 1, you're already well on your way to becoming a resilient boss who can perform well under pressure. To develop your resiliency further, here are steps to consider:

1. Understand the meaning of your work (#70) and have a clear view of your personal goals (#3). These "anchors" provide the sense of direction you need to make good decisions under pressure and help you develop self-confidence and self-efficacy (#4).

2. Develop the skills you need to cope well under pressure. First, you need to develop robust job- or profession-related skills so you are able to make the right decisions in difficult circumstances and develop the self-efficacy to work comfortably under pressure.

   Second, you need to work on your social and psychological skills, including thinking positively and managing negative thoughts (#6), managing stress well (#15), managing pressure (#17), solving problems effectively (Chapter 6), and increasing your emotional intelligence (#53). These techniques will help you overcome common stresses and disruptions in the workplace.

3. Build a strong support network at home and at work. When times are hard, it's incredibly important to be able to talk about issues with your partner, your boss, or your peers. They can provide emotional support – for example, by putting problems into perspective – and they can take practical actions to help you through difficult situations. (Of course, you won't be able to call on a network if you haven't nurtured it yourself beforehand – Chapters 16 and 18 will help you do this.)

4. Get the sleep, exercise, and nutrition you need to stay healthy. Exercise is particularly important as it helps to reduce stress, increases energy levels, and sharpens your ability to think and learn.

Finally, bear in mind the possibility that adversity can make us stronger. This "post-traumatic growth" occurs when something goes wrong for an individual and they make an honest, humble attempt to learn from what happened and what they might have done wrong, perhaps by talking things over with trusted people or by reflecting themselves (see #5). People can end up happier, wiser, and more successful as a result.

Find out more about resiliency, and download our resiliency
worksheet: http://mnd.tools/14-1
Learn more about post-traumatic growth: http://mnd.tools/14-2

15. Analyze and Manage Sources of Stress (Stress Diaries)

Stress is what we experience when we feel out of control and when we sense that the demands on us – emotional pressure, workload, or the complexity of what we're doing – are greater than our ability to deal with them. Even highly resilient people can suffer from stress. And needless to say, a high level of stress is dangerous – it can make us ill, it dampens our creativity, and it can make us difficult and volatile to work with. This can lead to even more stress as those around us often withdraw their cooperation and support, resulting in things getting even worse.

So, if you're experiencing stress, what can you do about it? The starting point is to understand where it's coming from, and a good way of doing this is to keep a stress diary.

This is a log of the stress events in your life, kept for a short period – maybe one or two weeks. You can record events when they happen, or you can set a timer on your smartphone to go off, say every two hours, so that you can record the stress events that have occurred in the previous two hours. (You can download a stress diary template using the URL on the following page.)

In your stress diary, record the following:

◆ The date and time of the stress event
◆ A brief description of the event
◆ How intense the stress you experienced was and how it left you feeling
◆ What you think caused the event.

Once you've collected data for a few weeks, you can analyze it by highlighting the most common sources of stress and also the most unpleasant events. These are the ones you should address first. See below to find out how to manage the different types of stress you've identified – you'll need to use different approaches for different situations.

> ## Important
>
> Stress can cause severe health problems and, in extreme cases, death. Seek the advice of a qualified health professional if you have any concerns over signs of ill health or if stress is causing you significant or persistent unhappiness.

Find out more about what stress is, and learn how to
manage it: http://mnd.tools/15-1

Find out more about stress diaries, and download our
template: http://mnd.tools/15-2

Access more than 80 tools that can help you manage the
stress in your life: http://mnd.tools/15-3

16. Manage Negative Emotions at Work (The STOP Method for Anger Management)

Just as we feel stressed when situations get out of control, we can also find ourselves getting angry. Anger is a primitive, natural reaction that we all experience when we think that we, or people important to us, are under threat.

In survival situations, this can be useful – anger primes our bodies for fast, vigorous action, and this can help us survive. In the workplace, however, anger damages the relationships that are necessary for success and leaves people looking foolish and out of control. It also hinders our ability to build a good team: Who wants to work with someone – particularly a boss – who shouts and can't control their temper?

So how can we control the natural anger we experience when we feel threatened, when we're thwarted, or when we experience or see injustice? The STOP technique for anger management is one useful approach. It stands for stop, think, be objective, and plan.

Stop – Reflect on the triggers, people, and things that cause you to become angry, and become aware of the warning signs– perhaps your breathing gets heavier or more rapid, your muscles tighten, your heart starts to race, or your voice gets louder. (If you're keeping a journal (#5), note these things in it to help you build up a picture of what's going on.)

Be alert to these signs of impending anger. When you find yourself starting to experience them, tell yourself: Stop! Sit down, take 10 deep breaths, and relax your body. (You can learn some useful relaxation techniques using the URL below.)

Think – Use a similar approach to the cognitive restructuring tool we looked at in #6 to reflect on the beliefs that led you to become angry. Write down a description of the situation, along with the "hot thoughts" you are experiencing. Then, examine rationally whether the threat is real and whether you are right to be getting angry. For example, if you're getting cross because a personal belief is being challenged, does your belief stand up to fair, balanced scrutiny?

Be objective – This is where you need to come to a clear, dispassionate view of the situation. Identify what is really going on: Is there a problem you need to solve, and if so, what is it?

Plan – If there is a problem, then you need to create a plan to solve it. Chapters 6 and 14 of this book will help you do this in highly effective ways, including giving you techniques for handling the tricky conversations that may be involved.

Find out more about anger management, and download our
anger management worksheet: http://mnd.tools/16-1

Learn some useful relaxation techniques: http://mnd.tools/16-2

Source: Adapted from Nay 2014. Reproduced with permission of Guilford Press.

17. Manage the Impact of Pressure on Performance (The Inverted–U Model)

We've seen that we need to develop resiliency and manage our stress levels to perform effectively at work. We also need to manage the amount of pressure we experience so that we can work in a "sweet

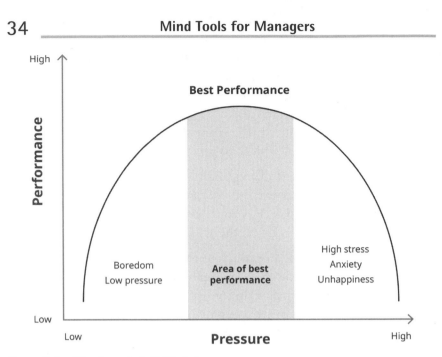

High

Performance

Low

Best Performance

Boredom

Low pressure

Area of best performance

High stress

Anxiety

Unhappiness

Low

High

Pressure

FIGURE **3.1** **The Inverted–U Model**

Source: Corbett 2015. Reproduced with permission of Emerald Publishing Ltd.

spot" where there's enough to motivate us to do a good job but not so much that we lose focus.

Research suggests that there is an inverted-U-shaped relationship between pressure and performance (see Figure 3.1), an idea that has helped athletes, businesspeople, and high achievers in many areas deliver exceptional performance.

The concept is straightforward. The area to the left of the graph is an area of poor performance – where people feel no pressure to perform, and struggle to motivate themselves. The area to the right of the graph is another area of poor performance – where people are overloaded, anxious, and so swamped by unhappy mental chatter that they can't focus. In-between is the sweet spot – where people can enter the state of flow we mentioned in #12 – the enjoyable and highly productive state of mind where nothing distracts them, their mind is completely focused on the work they're doing, and time flies by.

When you're working on something important, you can manage the pressure you're experiencing to move into this area of peak performance. If the pressure is low, you can remind yourself of the importance of the task and set challenges to generate interest and a buzz of achievement. If pressure is too high, you can calm yourself with deep breathing, use relaxation techniques, address negative thinking (see #6) and put the situation in context – few situations are genuinely as catastrophic as they seem when you're under pressure; there's often "another day."

Just as you can do these things for yourself, you can do them for members of your team. Try to gauge the level of pressure they are experiencing, and look for ways to fine tune it – for example, by reducing or lengthening the deadline for completing a task.

Tip

Don't confuse pressure with stress here – stress is about feeling out of control, and it's a harmful thing. You mustn't ever consciously raise stress levels – it can damage people's health, and it will be harmful to the way people see you.

Find out more about the inverted-U model:	http://mnd.tools/17-1
Discover more about flow:	http://mnd.tools/17-2

18. Overcome Fears of Failure or Success

Being resilient, managing pressure and stress, and controlling anger are all obvious skills that we need to master to be effective managers. In addition, many of the people who answered our survey highlighted the subtler skills of overcoming fear of failure and fear of success.

Fear of failure occurs when people who are able to achieve something challenging withdraw from it because, rather than risk falling short, they'd prefer to not make the attempt. People who fear failure don't stretch themselves and generally live a much less fulfilled life than they otherwise would. It's often observed in people who, in childhood, were punished seriously for failure and received little encouragement for success.

Fear of success is different, and it comes when people under-achieve, often because they fear rejection from people who are important to them if they were to stand out from the crowd. It's something that's quite common in people who doubt themselves or for whom having a lot of friends is more important than achievement.

When you reflect on your own career to date, have fears of failure or success held you back from achieving something significant? And if so, what can you do about it?

Start by reflecting on the situations where you have felt these things, write them down, and then make a note about what your thoughts and worries were for each. Use cognitive restructuring (#6) to challenge the thoughts that went with them.

When you review these situations in a balanced way, some of your concerns will just not stand up to rational scrutiny, and they'll drop away. But you may also highlight genuine issues and risks, and you'll need to deal with these in a calm, measured way. Make appropriate plans to deal with them – perhaps you'll need to learn new skills or build new connections that will move you forward.

When addressing fear of failure, it's usually enough to ask your-self: What is the worst that will happen if you fail? Usually, it is not a genuine catastrophe. And the risks of failure diminish when you take a "portfolio approach" to the things you do and the projects you run. You may not succeed at the first few things you try, but as long as you keep taking on new projects and giving them your best shot, some will succeed, and you can keep building on these to reach greater success.

When addressing fear of success, it *is* genuinely possible that the people around you may reject you if you succeed. But ask your-self if these are the people you should be spending time with. How much better would it be if you spent time with people who sup-ported you in your success and who encouraged you and helped you get ahead?

Discover more ways of dealing with fear of failure, and download our fear of failure worksheet:	http://mnd.tools/18-1
Discover more ways of dealing with fear of success, and download our fear of success worksheet:	http://mnd.tools/18-2

19. Learn from Your Experience in a Systematic Way (Gibbs's Reflective Cycle)

So far in this chapter, we've looked at specific issues – resiliency, stress, anger, pressure, and fears of success and failure. But what about all of the broader emotional issues and situations that we experience at work?

It is very useful to learn how to make sense of these situations, and this is where Gibbs's reflective cycle can help. Not only does it help us get to the root of tricky emotional situations, but it's also useful for helping us learn from general experience. This is something we all claim to do, but few of us do it as effectively and systematically as we might think.

Developed by Professor Graham Gibbs in his book *Learning by Doing*, the reflective cycle is particularly useful for helping people learn from situations that they experience regularly, especially when they don't go well. It encourages people to analyze these situations systematically and to maximize the benefits of their learning. You can see the cycle in Figure 3.2.

To use the cycle, start with the situation you want to reflect on, and go through these steps (use the URL on the next page to download a worksheet that will help you with this):

1. **Write a clear description of what happened.** Don't make any judgments at this stage – just describe what happened in a clear, factual way.

2. **Describe your feelings.** Write down all the emotions you experienced in the situation to get them out of your head and onto paper. Again, don't analyze or interpret them at this stage.

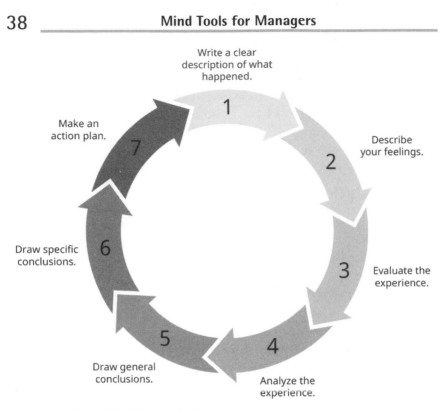

Write a clear description of what happened.

1

Make an action plan.

7

2

Describe your feelings.

Draw specific conclusions.

6

3

Evaluate the experience.

5

4

Draw general conclusions.

Analyze the experience.

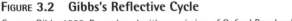

Figure 3.2   Gibbs's Reflective Cycle

Source: Gibbs 1988. Reproduced with permission of Oxford Brookes University.

3. **Evaluate the experience.** Using your intuition, write down your judgments about what was good or bad about the experience. What went well, what didn't go well, and what did you and other people do to contribute to this?

4. **Analyze the experience.** Now, switch from an emotional perspective into an analytical mindset, and think about what was really going on in the situation. (This is where a technique such as the five whys can help – see the URL on the next page for more on this.)

5. **Draw general conclusions.** Reflect on the previous steps, and start to think about things that could be done better and in a more positive way.

6. **Draw specific conclusions.** Then burrow into the detail of what you need to do to improve your ways of working, boost your skills, or change your situation for the better.

7. **Make an action plan.** Finally, turn your conclusions into specific actions you'll take, and add these to your to-do list or action program (see #10).

Find out more about Gibbs's reflective cycle, and download
a worksheet that will help you through these steps:　　　http://mnd.tools/19-1

Discover more about the five whys:　　　http://mnd.tools/19-2

Other Techniques for Coping with Change and Stress

There was one particularly important tool – avoiding maladaptive perfectionism – that missed the cut in our survey. You can learn more about it here: http://mnd.tools/c3c.

Chapter 4

Manage Your Career over Time

In society today, the work we do and the careers we pursue are central to our identity as individuals. When you are introduced to someone at a cocktail reception and they ask, "So what do you do?" it is assumed that they want to know about your work, not your family life or your hobbies.

But it is only in the past 200 years that this view of work as a key component of self-identity has become the norm. In the nineteenth century and earlier, people worked as a means of surviving, often in tedious activities such as farming or manufacturing. It was the privilege of the wealthy few to *not* have a job and to have time for enjoyable leisure activities.

Gradually, as society became wealthier and as technology allowed many basic jobs to be automated, the number of different jobs and careers multiplied. Today, work is at the center of our self-identity, and this means we put a great deal of effort into making sure we are doing worthwhile work. In Maslow's famous hierarchy of needs, the top of the hierarchy is self-actualization, and for people in developed countries with stable jobs, this notion that we should be seeking self-actualizing, or intrinsically motivating, work is a powerful driver.

In this chapter, we therefore examine a range of tools and techniques that you can use to help make your current work more enjoyable and to help you shape your future work and long-term career in a self-actualizing way.

First, we discuss the identity transition process (#20) to help you shift your career – especially if you are midcareer – in a direction that gives you greater satisfaction. We then describe three tools to help you assess and shape your choice of work, whatever stage you're at in your career: Finding a role that provides meaning and pleasure and plays to your strengths (#21), crafting an existing job so that it better suits your strengths and aspirations (#22), and understanding and enhancing the attributes that allow you to thrive at work (#23).

We then discuss the broader issues of work–life balance (#24), and we finish by looking at the major "career derailers" that often prevent people from realizing their ambitions (#25).

Although we fully endorse the idea that everyone should seek to get the most out of their work, one downside to this link between work and self-identity is that we often set unreasonably high expectations for ourselves. Some people seem to have a "calling" in life – a career that perfectly fits their skills and motivations – but that is quite rare. For most people, the challenge of finding interesting and enjoyable work is a never-ending pursuit. This underlines the importance of the techniques described here to help you periodically revisit the nature of the work you are doing and the future career choices you should be making.

20. Find a Career That Suits Who You Are (Ibarra's Identify Transition Process)

Although a few people are lucky enough to have a clear calling, the majority of us don't know what direction to head in as we enter the world of work. And once we have made our initial choices, we find it hard to step back or to reevaluate our options. The net result is that many people end up in careers that don't suit who they are. This leads them to perform in a mediocre way and leaves them feeling unfulfilled by their work.

If you have yet to start work, it's important to take career advice and use appropriate psychometric tests to identify the types of job you naturally gravitate to. And if you're early in your career, it's often easy to reflect on what interests you and follow well-established development paths that move you to the next natural career stage.

The problem is that people often reach a stage where they've been successful, where they've built strong skills, qualifications, and experience in a particular field, and where they have good salaries that reflect this. However, they feel like "birds in a gilded cage" – trapped in a good situation but not feeling fulfilled. It can be tempting to jump into an entirely different career, but we may find that this new career suits us no better than the one we've left behind.

This is where Herminia Ibarra's identity transition process is useful. She argues that our working identities are not fixed – they are made up of the many possible things that we could do, the many different people we could know and interact with, and the stories we tell ourselves about who we are. So, if we end up at a point where we are not satisfied with our career direction, we should take our time to try out – on a small scale – new types of work and new networks of people until we find what really suits who we are. Only then should we transition to that career.

To use the identity transition process (Figure 4.1), start off by asking, "Who might I become?" and from this, brainstorm interesting possibilities.

Choose the most exciting of these options, and then set up "crafting experiments" where you try out new types of work and new roles on a small scale to see whether they suit you. Identify people who are the gatekeepers to this type of work, find role models who do it well, and identify the professional and peer networks that support it. Talk to these people to understand the day-to-day reality of the work and the qualifications and skills you need to succeed in it. Finally, with this new knowledge, think about the stories you tell yourself about yourself, and reflect on whether these have changed.

Take your time trying out these new types of work, and "linger between these identities." Try the new identities on, experience their upsides and downsides, and feel which of them suit you best.

Then reflect on what this tells you about yourself. Based on what you've learned, this may be the time to restart the cycle and think about and explore other possibilities.

Only when you find a career that suits you should you give up your current role and move into it.

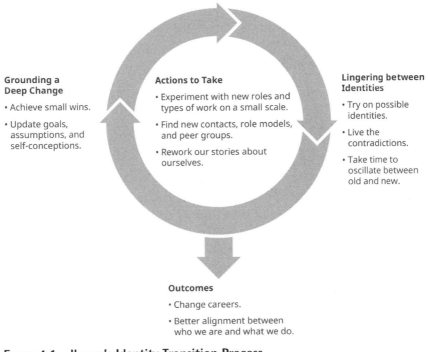

Exploring Possible Selves

• Ask "Who might I become?"

• List possibilities.

• Refine questions.

Grounding a Deep Change

• Achieve small wins.

• Update goals, assumptions, and self-conceptions.

Actions to Take

• Experiment with new roles and types of work on a small scale.

• Find new contacts, role models, and peer groups.

• Rework our stories about ourselves.

Lingering between Identities

• Try on possible identities.

• Live the contradictions.

• Take time to oscillate between old and new.

Outcomes

• Change careers.

• Better alignment between who we are and what we do.

FIGURE **4.1**   **Ibarra's Identity Transition Process**

Source: Ibarra 2003. Reproduced with permission of Harvard Business Publishing.

Tip

Remember that if you change to a career where none of your previous skills, experience, and connections are relevant, you'll be competing with career starters fresh out of educational institutions, and you may need to be on a similar salary scale to them. Try to keep your new role as close as you possibly can to your previous experience – that way, you can retain some of your previous salary.

Find out more about the identity transition process: http://mnd.tools/20

21. Find a Role That Provides Meaning and Pleasure and Fully Uses Your Strengths (The MPS Process)

Once you're in the right type of career, you need to find a specific role that builds on your talents and stretches you – in a good way. One useful way of doing this is to use the MPS process, developed by Harvard professor Dr. Tal Ben-Shahar. MPS stands for three important questions: (1) What gives me meaning? (2) What gives me pleasure? and (3) What uses my strengths?

To explore meaning, you can start by exploring your workplace values – the ways of working that you think are important for doing a good job (use the URL below to find out more about this). Ask yourself what roles and activities best fit with these values. Then, reflect on things that you have done that gave you the greatest sense of meaning. List these, and identify common factors.

Exploring pleasure is easy. Simply list the things you enjoy – hobbies, interests, and anything that brings you joy and contentment, and again, identify common factors. We looked at strengths as part of the personal SWOT (strengths, weaknesses, opportunities, and threats) analysis (#2).

Next, look for areas of overlap among your three lists to identify types of work that you find meaningful and enjoyable and that use your strengths. If some of these are obvious, then that's fantastic! However, if it's harder to find these things, explore areas where two of these areas overlap as well.

Finally, think about how you can move your career toward doing these types of work. We'll look how you can do this next by looking at job crafting.

Find out more about exploring your values:	http://mnd.tools/21-1
Learn more about the MPS process:	http://mnd.tools/21-2

22. Shape Your Role to Suit Your Strengths and Aspirations (Job Crafting)

Job crafting involves making subtle changes to the way that you do your job so that your work fits your strengths and gives you the emotional reward and human connection you want.

This sounds difficult. We have objectives we need to achieve and expectations from those around us, all of which limit our freedom to make changes. However, there are usually things you can work on to tweak or "craft" your job so that you are still delivering on all your objectives but doing so in a way that brings you greater meaning and intrinsic satisfaction. There are four main ways that Amy Wrzesniewski and Jane Dutton, who first discussed job crafting, say you can do this:

1. **By subtly changing the activities you do** – Your job description will list things you need to do, and you need to do these well. But there is often scope for changing how you do them. By taking initiative and applying your own personal talents to your work, you can often lift the quality and impact to a whole new level.

2. **By changing the number of activities you do** – You might try to increase your workload in an area you enjoy, perhaps by helping colleagues. If you're overloaded in other areas, you may be able to negotiate with your boss to do fewer of these things or get extra help.

3. **By increasing human contact, or changing the people you interact with** – Wrzesniewski and Dutton talk about hospital cleaners, who can either put their heads down and work without talking to anyone, or choose to be positive and helpful and fit their work around ward routines. The latter group contribute more to the successful running of a ward and get a lot more out of their jobs too.

4. **By changing how you see the job** – If hospital cleaners see their job as "just cleaning," they'll be tempted to cut corners and do the minimum. If they see their work as an important part of helping patients get better, it brings real meaning to what they do, and they will approach their work in a more thorough, careful way.

These changes are all quite small, but they can make a big difference to your job satisfaction and to your success. What's more, you usually don't need permission for such changes – you just get on and make them.

Find out more about job crafting, including how to do it: http://mnd.tools/22

23. Thrive at Work (The GREAT DREAM Model)

We've looked at how you can navigate into and craft a role that suits who you are. A final step in flourishing in the workplace is to find ways to enrich the day-to-day work you do, and this is where the GREAT DREAM model can help. Developed by Vanessa King in her book *10 Keys to Happier Living,* GREAT DREAM stands for 10 key things that help people find happiness in their everyday lives, including at work:

1. **Giving (G)** – Whether it's complimenting a coworker who's done a good job, buying cookies for your team, or helping someone who's struggling, being kind to others can help us enjoy work too. Partly, this is practical – our relationships improve, and people respond thoughtfully to us as a consequence. However, we're also "wired" to give – being generous releases feel-good neurotransmitters into our brain, helping us feel happier and less stressed.

2. **Relating (R)** – We define ourselves in large part through the people we know and interact with, and strong personal relationships are crucially important for our sense of happiness and well-being at work. We look at what you can do to build great relationships at work in #63.

3. **Exercising (E)** – We all know that we need to exercise for health reasons. However, regular exercise helps us deal with stress better, and it promotes neuroplasticity – helping our brains stay healthy, adaptable, and sharp as we age. The link below will help you find ways to build exercise into a busy schedule.

4. **Awareness (A)** – In this context, awareness means mindfulness, and we'll touch on aspects of this in #50 when we look at mindful listening. Mindfulness can help you experience life more intensely at the same time that you manage stress better. Again, you can find out more about it using the link below.

5. **Trying out (T)** – This is about being curious and creative and trying new things. We all love to learn and grow as

individuals, and we need to make sure that there are plenty of opportunities to do this in our work.

6. **Direction (D)** – We saw the importance of personal goals in #3. Direction comes from having clear goals, pursued in an open, optimistic frame of mind.

7. **Resiliency (R)** – A key part of being happy at work is resiliency (#14) – being able to "bounce back" quickly and effectively from the setbacks we inevitably encounter, rather than dwelling on them.

8. **Emotions (E)** – As we've already seen, emotions really matter at work. If we and people around us behave in a positive, emotionally intelligent (#53) way, we can all be so much happier, more creative, and more successful in our work.

9. **Acceptance (A)** – This is about being as compassionate to ourselves as we are to our closest friends. A lot of this comes down to capitalizing on our own strengths (#2) and listening to our own thoughts and challenging them when our self-judgments are harsh and unhelpful (#6).

10. **Meaning (M)** – We all crave some sort of meaning in our lives, a sense that our existence or our work is linked to a higher purpose (see #21). Sometimes we get this meaning through our religion or through being part of a thriving local community. But we can also get it through work. Many businesses serve an important or noble purpose in society, and if this purpose is one you can relate to, you will typically be more fulfilled and effective.

The 10 elements of GREAT DREAM matter to varying degrees to different people. So go through each of the headings. Think about how much each element matters to you, and brainstorm how you can bring more of this into your daily life. For example, if your relationship with your children gives you a lot of pleasure, put photos of them on your desk. If personal relationships are important for you, invite coworkers to lunch.

Add these changes to your action program (#10.) Even small tweaks can make a huge difference to your sense of happiness and well-being.

Find out more about how you can use the GREAT DREAM model at work:	http://mnd.tools/23-1
Discover how to fit exercise into a busy schedule:	http://mnd.tools/23-2
Learn more about mindfulness at work:	http://mnd.tools/23-3

Source: Adapted from King 2016. Reproduced with permission of Headline Publishing.

24. Find the Work–Life Balance That's Best for You (The Wheel of Life®)

In this chapter, we've looked at how you can navigate your way into a role that suits you, and we've seen how to shape it so that you can truly flourish at work. But what about life outside work? We've all heard about the spectacularly successful CEO who missed seeing his children grow up or the hard-working production manager who dropped dead after a heart attack at 48 years of age.

The wheel of life is a useful tool to help you find the right balance between your work and personal lives and was developed by Paul J. Meyer. It helps you explore what's important in your life and think about how much satisfaction you're experiencing in each area.

To draw a wheel of life (Figure 4.2), start by downloading the template or using the interactive tool you'll find at the URL below. Then take these steps:

1. Brainstorm the areas of life that are important to you. These could be the roles you want to play, such as being a good partner, parent, friend, or boss, or they could be different areas of life, such as career, self-development, or artistic expression. Identify the most important of these, and label the spokes of your wheel with them.

2. Plot points on each spoke showing where each would be in your ideal life, and join these up to show its "shape." These should not all be at the maximum level – some things will always matter to you more than others. (In Figure 4.2, the black line shows this ideal shape for the person drawing the wheel.)

3. Plot points on each spoke for where things are now, and join these points up. This shows the shape of your current life. (This is shown by the dotted line in the example in Figure 4.2.)

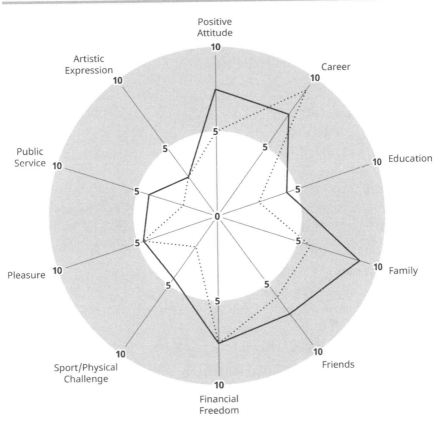

Figure 4.2   **Example Wheel of Life**
Source: Paul J. Meyer.

4. The gaps between your "current" and "ideal" lives are where you need to take action. Where specific areas are getting less attention than you'd ideally want, plan how you'll change this. Equally, where you're putting in more effort than you want, think about how to reduce your effort in those areas. Add these points to your action program (#10).

Download the wheel of life template, or use the interactive tool: http://mnd.tools/24

25. Understand the Types of Behavior That Can Derail Your Career (Hogan Management Derailment)

We have discussed various ways of identifying and building on your strengths as a way of making work more fulfilling. But this approach comes with a warning: Things that appear to be strengths in the short term can become weaknesses in the long term when taken too far and can result in career derailment. This happens more often than you might think.

Career derailment has been studied for many years by psychologists and doctors Robert and Joyce Hogan. Look through the areas below for strengths that you might have; then think about and guard against the associated weaknesses – they can be career killers:

Excitability – People strong on excitability have lots of energy and enthusiasm, but, under pressure, they can be moody, unpredictable, and easily annoyed. It can be hard to work with them because you never know what to expect.

Skepticism – Skeptical people are often smart and politically astute, but they can look too hard for deceit or betrayal, and they can become mistrustful and argumentative when under stress. Others can find them difficult and can be afraid of retaliation if they say something "wrong."

Cautiousness – These people can be a "safe pair of hands," but they can also be resistant to change and risk, and others may see them as unassertive, slow, and pessimistic. They can slow an organization down and cause it to miss opportunities.

Reservedness – People who are reserved can often be tough and determined under pressure, but they are often poor listeners and they can become uncommunicative as stress develops. People who work with them can see them as uncaring, inconsiderate, and self-centered.

Leisureliness – Leisurely people are easy to get along with, and they seem to work cooperatively and productively. However, they can be stubborn, they can procrastinate, and they can be resentful toward others. People who work with them may find them passive-aggressive and mean.

Boldness – These people are full of self-confidence. However, they often focus on the positives and ignore the negatives, and they may blame others for their own failings. People who work with them can see such people as opinionated and demanding when it comes to decision making.

Mischievousness – These people can be bright, charming risk takers, but they can be dishonest, ignore rules, exploit others, and focus on short-term gains despite long-term pain. All of this can cause huge damage.

Colorfulness – People who score high on this dimension are entertaining, engaging, and well-liked. However, they can be easily distracted, and their work is often disorganized. All of this can make them difficult to work with.

Imaginativeness – Imaginative people think creatively and can adopt unique perspectives on issues and problems. Some of their ideas are brilliant, but others are fanciful. Such people often lack common sense and make poor decisions.

Diligence – Conscientiousness, reliability, and attention to detail are key characteristics of diligent people. However, they expect others to be as hardworking as they are. They often struggle with delegation, and people who work with them can feel disenchanted because their work is always being redone.

Dutifulness – These people are considerate, easy to deal with, and great team players. However, they can also be "people pleasers" who work for approval and hold back on expressing contrary opinions. You can't depend on them for critical thinking because they may just accept and go along with bad ideas.

Hogan and Hogan have compiled a test – sometimes known as the "dark side test" – that helps you spot these problems and neutralize them before they run amok. You can find out more about this using the URL below.

Find out more about the Hogan development survey:	http://mnd.tools/25

Source: Adapted from Hogan, Hogan, and Kaiser 2011. Reproduced with permission of the American Psychological Association.

Other Techniques for Managing Your Career

The tools covered in this chapter and recommended in our survey are good, classic approaches to career development. It's also worth exploring the ideas of Marcus Buckingham and Marshall Goldsmith. Learn more at http://mnd.tools/c4c.

Part II

Manage Tasks, and Get Things Done

Chapter 5

Get Work Done in an Efficient and Focused Way

Perhaps your biggest responsibility as a manager, in terms of day-to-day priorities, is making sure work is done in an efficient and focused way. Of course, good managers are highly attuned to the "people" side of their job, as we discuss in later chapters, but the focus here is primarily on the efficient coordination and alignment of tasks. Think of the firm as a well-oiled machine, where everything links together in beautiful alignment – that is what you should be aiming for.

Unfortunately, most large firms are nothing like well-oiled machines, for two reasons. First, they are often so large and complex that people are oblivious to what is happening elsewhere, and senior executives – even with the best will in the world – struggle to provide a coherent message to everyone. Second, the bigger the firm, the further removed individual employees are from the fruits of their labor, and the harder it is to keep them motivated to continuously improve on their performance.

This chapter provides a set of tools and techniques you can use to improve efficiency and focus in day-to-day work. The first two are high-level techniques that you will partly be on the receiving end of, specifically translating the firm's mission into goals that people understand (#26) and aligning people's objectives with corporate goals (#27). The others are techniques that you should use with members of your teams to help achieve your objectives. Two are focused on efficiency – systematically analyzing and optimizing the work people do (#28) and using structured, continuous improvement methods (#29). Two are more concerned with effectiveness, i.e. doing the right things – identifying the "gaps" that need filling to achieve objectives (#30) and conducting post-project reviews to make sure you are prioritizing the right activities (#31). Finally, we provide an overview of agile methodologies for managing projects (#32) – agile is one of the hottest current trends in the business world, so it is important to be up to speed on how it works.

There is a long history of management research on the issues described in this chapter – for example, the original scientific management and time-and-motion studies of Fredrick Taylor, as well as the quality revolution inspired by Edwards Deming and first implemented by Toyota. Recent management innovations, including Six Sigma and agile development, build on these traditions. But though the terminology changes over time, the underlying need to create alignment and efficiency at work is timeless.

26. Translate the Organization's Mission into Goals That People Understand (OGSM)

We have already discussed how important it is to have meaning in your life and how different aspects of the way you work can contribute to this. An important part of meaning, though, comes from what your organization does to address the needs of its stakeholders. This is typically expressed in a mission or vision statement that provides what Ratan Tata, former CEO of Tata Sons, calls a "spiritual and moral call to action." (See #81 for more on mission statements.)

But it is often difficult to see how the work we do, day to day, contributes to the organization's mission. Or to put it slightly differently, it is hard for senior managers to translate higher-level objectives into individual targets without producing lengthy plans that people struggle to understand and that they quickly forget. This is where OGSMs (objectives, goals, strategies, and measures) are useful. Developed by Marc Van Eck and Ellen van Zanten in *The One Page Business Strategy* and used by many large companies, this framework brings together the full hierarchy of objectives used by the organization and summarizes them on a handy one-page sheet that everyone can make sense of. The one-page rule is great for pushing senior managers to make difficult decisions rather than lazy compromises. It's also great for communicating what people need to do in a clear and very condensed way.

The objective is a concise and emotionally appealing statement of what the organization is seeking to achieve. For example, your objective might be "to become the world leader in electric van manufacturing." You could expand on this by adding "by developing cutting-edge battery technology, high-performance motors, and an innovative workforce."

Goals are a small number of statements (typically three or four) of what success looks like. An example might be: "Within the next 12 months, develop a battery pack capable of giving a 10,000-pound vehicle a range of 650 miles."

Strategies are short descriptions of what you'll do to achieve your goal (this is a very particular meaning of the word *strategy* and different than how the term is used by others, as we'll discuss in Chapter 15.) An example might be: "Recruit a team of seven engineers with strong experience of developing and integrating specialist electric vehicle battery packs."

Measures are the specific quantitative things you'll monitor to check that your goals and strategies are being met. (These are often presented on a dashboard.)

Find out more about OGSMs, including downloading an
OGSM template: http://mnd.tools/26

Source: Adapted from van Eck and van Zanten 2014. Reproduced with permission of Marc van Eck and Ellen van Zanten.

27. Align People's Objectives with Corporate Goals (OKRs)

OGSMs are great for translating the organization's mission into actions for specific operating units or departments. But how can these goals and strategies be translated into the work that individuals do?

This is where OKRs (objectives and key results) are useful. Developed by Andy Grove, former CEO of Intel®, and widely used in leading organizations, they are a refinement of the notion of management by objectives, developed in the 1950s by Peter Drucker (which you can find out more about using the URL on the next page.)

Objectives define what someone needs to achieve during a defined period, and key results are measures of progress or milestones along the way to achieving them.

OKRs start at the top of the organization, and they are based on the business plan or OGSM. They cascade down from level to level so that, ultimately, every individual has personal objectives and key results that contribute to the OKRs of the manager above them.

So how are OKRs defined? Typically, your manager will gather a team together to discuss the overall plan. Then he or she will work with each individual and agree on the personal objectives that help deliver on the collective goal. Rather than simply tell people what to do, the manager should ask for each individual's insights into the goals being set, giving them the opportunity to discuss any problems they see and bid for any additional resources needed.

There are two types of objectives – operational and aspirational. Operational objectives are the first priority, and they either are achieved or not. Aspirational objectives – also known as stretch goals or "moon shots" – are a way of encouraging people to do something hugely significant.

For each objective, your manager will discuss and agree on two or three key results. These will either be measures showing whether they have been achieved or milestones that you'll need to reach along the way to achieving the objective. The two of you will then work out a structure of one-on-one meetings to review progress and quarterly meetings where you'll look at where you should be going next and how your OKRs might be adjusted.

Having done this with your manager, you then replicate the process with the people who report to you, and they do the same, until OKRs have rippled down through the whole organization.

Find out more about management by objectives:	http://mnd.tools/27-1
Learn more about OKRs, including seeing an example:	http://mnd.tools/27-2

Source: Adapted from Grove 1995. Reproduced with permission of Pearson Education, Inc.

28. Systematically Analyze and Optimize the Work Team Members Do (DILO)

With mature, experienced individuals, setting objectives may be all that you need to do to get them working well. With less experienced team members, though, you often need to get more involved, which means understanding the detail of the work they are doing.

By getting into the detail, you become knowledgeable about what is happening in your team, you can help people to focus on the right things, and you can assess their need for additional training and resources. You will also come to understand who you can rely on to work with minimal supervision and who you need to manage closely.

A useful technique for doing this is DILO, which stands for day in the life of. It was originally developed as a way to understand customers' lives, but it is equally useful for understanding what's going on in your team.

It involves tracking the details of what people are doing over a period of time and then analyzing this to improve efficiency. There is a risk of appearing overbearing and intrusive in this activity, which could, in turn, generate resentment and resistance, but when done right, it can make life better for everyone. An example of a completed DILO analysis for an airport worker is in Figure 5.1.

Start your DILO analysis by defining its scope. For how long do you want to run the analysis? What parts of your team's work do you want it to apply to? And for what purpose – do you want to identify training needs, fix problems that team members are experiencing, or explore new ways of doing things that might be useful?

Communicate this to the people involved. Explain what you want to achieve and why and, most importantly, make it clear that you won't be using this process to judge them – otherwise, they'll be suspicious about what you're trying to achieve.

Time	Duration	Core Activity	Activity Category	Effectiveness Rating (1–5)
06:00	5 mins	Signing in and registering for the job.	Admin	3
06:05	10 mins	Walking from team room to Gate 27.	Transit time	5
06:15	10 mins	Calling the flight; setting up the boarding of the flight on the system; checking in with Movement Control.	Flight setup	4
06:25	5 mins	Discussing specifics of the boarding with airline rep and dispatches rep.	Flight setup	4

FIGURE 5.1 **Part of an Example DILO Analysis for an Airport Worker**

Next, set up the time recording worksheet – a simple time log noting the time the activity starts, what the activity is, how long the person takes to do it, and a rating of how effective the person feels they are being. It is often best to ask people to complete the log themselves – this gives them control over the situation.

When the study is complete, review the time logs with the individual. Make sure you are clear what each task is. Where someone feels they weren't doing the job as effectively as they might, explore the reasons (for example, using the five whys; see the URL below).

If done sensitively, this gives you the starting point for some great conversations about addressing frustrations, solving equipment issues, improving processes, and so on. Make sure to keep your promise not to judge the person being studied.

Find out more about how to do a DILO analysis, including
downloading a DILO worksheet: http://mnd.tools/28-1

Find out more about the five whys: http://mnd.tools/28-2

---

29. Use a Structured Approach to Continuous Improvement (PDSA)

PDSA (plan, do, study, and act) is another technique you can use to improve the way your team works in a systematic and controlled way. It is a scientific approach to continuous improvement: Develop a hypothesis for improving a process, try it out, assess whether it is supported, and act on the findings.

Developed by W. Edwards Deming in the 1950s, PDSA became a core part of the wave of lean manufacturing and quality improvement movements, which reshaped global industries in the subsequent decades. It was developed in a manufacturing context and is now widely used in any situation where process improvement is important. (PDSA was originally known as PDCA, but Deming asked for the acronym to be changed after it caused confusion.) It follows the cycle shown in Figure 5.2.

In the plan phase, you focus on a problem to understand its underlying causes (use the five whys and cause and effect diagrams

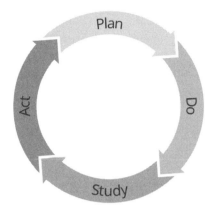

Figure 5.2   The PDSA Cycle

(#34) to do this effectively). You develop a hypothesis saying what you think the problem is and state quantitatively what your expectations are if it is resolved. You brainstorm options for resolving the problem, select the solution you want to test, and plan how to run the test, ideally on a small-scale basis first.

In the do phase, you carry out your plan and collect the data you need to assess whether expectations have been met.

In the study phase (originally called check), you study the data to see whether the problem has been solved. If yes, you move on to the act phase; if no, you return to the plan phase.

In the act phase, you roll your changes out fully and embed them in the organization's way of working. (This can be harder than you might initially think – see Chapter 17 for more on change management skills.)

You can then move back to the start of the cycle and identify the next improvement you want to work on.

Tips

◆ PDSA works particularly well as part of *kaizen*, an approach to continuous improvement that often focuses on the elimination of different types of waste. Use the URL on the following page to find out more.

◆ PDSA is similar to an approach called build-measure-learn, which focuses on building a "minimum viable product" to test hypotheses in fast-moving, uncertain environments such as the tech sector. You can find out more about this using the URL below.

Find out more about how to use PDSA/PDCA: http://mnd.tools/29-1

Learn about *kaizen*:   http://mnd.tools/29-2

Find out how to use the build-measure-learn cycle: http://mnd.tools/29-3

30. Systematically Identify What Needs to Be Done – Gap Analysis

To make changes such as those in the do phase of PDSA or to meet other objectives, you will often need to run projects – temporary streams of work with clear start and end points. An important part of setting a project up is defining what work you'll do in it, and this is where gap analysis is useful.

Gap analysis is simply about defining the space between your current state (where you are now) and the desired future state you want to achieve and then figuring out what work needs to be done to close the gap. Take the following steps:

1. **Define the scope of the project.** Define what your project will and won't cover. Try to keep the scope small and focused – larger projects have a tendency to run out of control.
2. **Identify the desired future state.** For the chosen activity, define where you want to end up. For example, if you are building a website, define what success looks like in terms of visual quality, hits, click-through rates, etc.
3. **Identify the current state.** Next, put together a frank assessment of the current state of play, consulting with others as necessary. If you already have a prototype website, how would you rate it on the relevant quantitative indicators you have chosen?

4. **Identify how to bridge the gaps.** It may be obvious what actions you need to take to bridge the gap between the current state and the future state, but in more complex situations, it is often worth using cause and effect analyses (#34) or brainstorming (#48) to generate alternatives.

As an example of a gap analysis, you could define the scope of your project as "shortening the resolution time for customers making inquiries through your website." Your desired future state could be "to solve 85% of customer issues within 2 hours of their inquiry and 100% within 24 hours while maintaining a 93% or higher satisfaction rate." Your current state could be: "We solve 85% of customer issues within 8 hours of their inquiry and 100% within 24 hours with a 93% satisfaction level." Cause and effect analysis allows you to explore why you are not achieving the desired service levels and identify possible ways forward.

Tips

◆ When you're doing a gap analysis, it's easy to focus on process changes and neglect the people side of the story. The McKinsey seven Ss model is useful for keeping all the relevant dimensions of the organization in mind. Find out more about this using the URL below.

◆ When you do gap analysis, you'll often find the project is too expensive. If this happens, work through the elements that make up the project using the MoSCoW method – identifying must haves, should haves, could haves, and won't haves. Follow the URL below to learn more.

Learn more about gap analysis:	http://mnd.tools/30-1
Find out more about the McKinsey seven Ss model:	http://mnd.tools/30-2
Learn how to use the MoSCoW method:	http://mnd.tools/30-3

31. Conduct Post–Completion Project Reviews (Retrospectives)

DILO and PDCA are good techniques for getting work done more *efficiently*. When you couple them with OGSM and OKRs, you'll be working in a much more effective way as well – by focusing on the right things. You can do even better when you put a formal "learning from experience" step into how your team works, and you can do this by running *retrospectives* at the end of projects.

Retrospectives are a key feature of agile project management, and they are run at the end of each agile sprint, typically every two weeks. (We'll look at agile in more detail next in #32). They are also known as *after action reviews*, a term that has been used in the military world for many years.

The purpose of retrospectives is to get team members to take collective responsibility for learning from their recent experiences and improving the way they work the next time they encounter a similar challenge. These sessions need to be run promptly and in a non-hierarchical, blame-free way; otherwise, people will have forgotten the details of what happened or they may cover up things that went wrong for fear of looking bad.

Start by explaining the context and purpose. Make it clear that everyone is expected to contribute and that disagreement is okay as long as it is nonpersonal and constructive. Focus on the following questions:

1. What was supposed to happen? What did happen? Where and why was there a difference?
2. What didn't go well and why?
3. What did go well and why?
4. What will we stop doing, start doing, and keep doing to make the next project a success?

You can just let people talk and take notes, or you may prefer a more structured process – for example, getting people to write on sticky notes and putting them up on a chart for all to see. Depending on where you work, there may also be special templates that everyone uses.

Ultimately, you're looking to improve the way your team works – by improving training, codifying people's knowledge in key areas, or improving procedures and working methods. Make sure that you take down a list of actions coming out of the session and that you follow up on these to make sure they happen.

Find out more about how to run an after action review: http://mnd.tools/31-1

Learn how to run a retrospective, including different
approaches to use for them: http://mnd.tools/31-2

---

32. Manage Projects Using Agile Methodologies (Agile Project Management)

The previous two techniques (#30 and #31) addressed specific aspects of project management. But there is also the question of how to manage projects in their totality. Broadly speaking, there are two approaches available to you. Where the technologies used by the project are well understood, where the product is quite standardized and can be designed in detail (such as a house, a bridge, or a ship), and where it needs to be delivered to a tight budget and a defined timescale, a structured approach to project management such as PMBOK and PRINCE2 is useful; these allow projects to be delivered in a controlled and highly efficient way.

Unfortunately, this structured approach doesn't work well in many high-tech sectors where requirements are not well understood in advance, technologies are evolving quickly, and customer requirements are shifting. Highly structured project methodologies do not cope well with changing demands, and the net result is missed deadlines, cost overruns, and, often, a product that doesn't meet the evolving needs of the organization. Working on such projects can be stressful and demoralizing.

This is where Agile Project Management is useful. In essence, it replaces the top-down process where everything is planned in advance with a bottom-up process that adapts to the changing circumstances. It involves a trade-off: Customers and sponsors lose their right to know exactly when the project will be finished and how much the product will ultimately cost, but they gain a flexible and dynamic approach that starts delivering small, useful results almost from the start of the project, resulting in a product that meets the needs of the evolving organization.

One popular approach to agile project management is called *scrum*. Here, projects are built around small, self-directed teams where team members work together in short bursts of activity called *sprints*. These are typically two to four weeks in length, and the aim is for the project team to deliver a small, fully tested, working deliverable by the end of each sprint.

Within the teams, there are several key roles. *Product owners* act as representatives of customers and end users. Before each sprint, they reprioritize the order in which deliverables will be worked on and describe how the deliverables will be used through a format called a *user story*. At the end of the sprint, product owners confirm that the team has successfully delivered a solution to the user stories being worked on.

Scrum masters manage the process of each sprint. They break the user story down into smaller user stories that can be completed within the sprint, protect the project team from scope creep, help to solve problems within the sprint, and conduct project retrospectives (see #31) at the end of each sprint to identify lessons learned so that these can be fed into future ones.

Agile coaches are the third key role – these individuals provide support to several teams, helping with personal development and offering advice on team dynamics.

Project team members decide which user stories can be completed within the sprint, and they self-organize to develop a working solution for each one by the end of the sprint. Team members meet at the start of the sprint to decide how this will be done and then hold 15-minute stand-up meetings every day to update one another on progress.

When it is used effectively, this agile approach gives senior managers a high level of visibility over the progress of the projects they are responsible for, and it gives project team members more autonomy and greater opportunities for personal development. However, it is not that easy to use: You need to invest a lot of time building the new structures and developing the skills needed to put it into practice.

Notes

- ◆ PMBOK, PRINCE2, and Agile are complex methodologies. We can give only a flavor of them here, and you'll need formal training to use them effectively. The links below take you to the standards and training bodies responsible for them.
- ◆ Unlike the other techniques in this book, which were identified as important by our survey of 15,000 managers and professionals, agile is included because we, as authors, thought it was important. Adoption of agile methodologies is accelerating rapidly, so you need to understand them.

Learn more about PMBOK (pmi.org):	http://mnd.tools/32-1
Find out more about PRINCE2 (axelos.com):	http://mnd.tools/32-2
Learn how to use agile project management (Mountain Goat Software):	http://mnd.tools/32-3
Learn how to use agile project management (Scrum Alliance):	http://mnd.tools/32-4

Chapter 6

Solve Problems Effectively

One of your central tasks as a manager is to resolve problems. In a problem-free workplace, where everyone got their work done fluidly and seamlessly, there would be little need for managers at all.

Problems come in all shapes and sizes, and the way they should be handled varies accordingly. The last chapter, in fact, included several techniques, such as PDSA (plan, do, study, and act) cycles and agile working methods, which are useful for resolving small run-of-the-mill problems. But sometimes problems are much more substantial, causing a production line to break down, a deadline to be missed, or an important customer relationship to be mishandled. In these cases, you need a different set of techniques, and that is what we are looking at here.

Three of these techniques are about digging into visible problems to unearth the reasons they occurred in the first place: These are getting systematically to the root of a problem (#33), identifying the many possible causes of a problem (#34), and mapping business processes clearly (#35). Then we take an unusual perspective, namely solving problems by capitalizing on what's going well (#36). Finally, we discuss a people-based approach that can be relevant to several of the other techniques, namely bringing people together to solve problems (#37).

A couple of important themes cut across all these techniques. First, your role as a manager is rarely to simply pinpoint the cause of a problem and implement the solution. More often, you are putting in place some sort of problem-solving process that taps into the insights and perspectives of others – partly because they will often be the ones who know the details and partly because their involvement will be needed to implement the chosen solution. So, even though problem solving is ultimately a task-focused activity, it typically needs quite a lot of social and diplomatic skill on your part if it is to work effectively.

And a word of caution: These techniques are great, but they all take time. If you are trying to unknot a problem that is holding everything up – for example, a broken-down production system – you may have no option but to get to the bottom of it. But there are other types of problems where you are trying to figure out a sensible way forward and there is no right or wrong answer. These are sometimes called "wicked problems." In such cases, there is a real risk of analysis paralysis – a desire to collect more data and to do an in-depth investigation just to make sure you are going the right way. Many large firms suffer from this pathology, and of course, it leads to finger-pointing, defensive behavior, and slow decision making.

So, although it is important to come to grips with all these problem-solving processes, you also need to keep in mind the cost and effort involved in using them. One of the hallmarks of good managers is knowing how much to intervene – sometimes a light touch is fine; at other times, a deep-dive problem-solving technique is what's needed.

33. Get Systematically to the Root of a Problem (Root Cause Analysis)

Sometimes, it's easy to pinpoint the cause of business problems, and you can quickly develop solutions. Other problems are particularly knotty, and despite a team's best efforts, they evade resolution. And then there are the serious problems with major downside risks where you need to get the solution right the first time.

These latter two cases are where a thorough process like root cause analysis is most useful. Use it to understand in detail what happened and to develop solutions so that it doesn't happen again.

There are typically three types of causes: physical causes, such as something breaking; human causes, such as someone not undertaking preventive maintenance; and organizational causes, such as hiring the wrong people, not making sufficient resources available, or departments acting at cross-purposes to each other. Although it is easy to blame individuals for not doing their jobs properly, the root cause is usually much deeper – there is typically some sort of organizational or procedural flaw that lies behind nonperformance. Here are the key steps in root cause analysis:

1. *Assemble a team of people* with the expertise needed to solve the problem. Some should have practical, day-to-day experience of the problem; others should have relevant technical expertise.

2. *Define the problem.* A tool such as CATWOE (customers–actors–transformation process–world view–owner and environmental constraints) can help here; see below for a link to it. This helps you view the problem from a range of perspectives and develop a well-crafted problem definition.

3. *Collect data.* Study the situation fully and in detail to understand what is going on, often by collecting additional data.

4. *Identify possible causal factors.* Use approaches such as cause and effect analysis (#34) and causal factor charting (see URL below) to discover possible causes.

5. *Identify root causes* by drilling into these possible causes; for example, using the five whys to help.

6. *Recommend and test solutions.* Some of these will obviously make sense and can be implemented right away. Others may be more tentative or may have consequences that need to be explored. This is where you can test them and implement them in a controlled way using an approach such as PDSA (see #29).

Find out more about CATWOE:	http://mnd.tools/33-1
Learn more about causal factor charting:	http://mnd.tools/33-2
Discover more about the five whys:	http://mnd.tools/33-3
Learn more about root cause analysis:	http://mnd.tools/33-4

34. Identify the Many Possible Causes of a Problem (Cause and Effect Analysis)

Cause and effect analysis is another popular framework that managers use to brainstorm the possible sources of a problem. Popularized in Japan in the 1960s by Professor Kaoru Ishikawa, it pushes you to explore all possible causes of a problem, rather than just the most obvious one, so that you are more likely to solve it the first time around. It is a technique that has stood the test of time.

Cause and effect analyses are often called *fishbone diagrams* because they look like the head and skeleton of a fish – see the example in Figure 6.1.

These diagrams are traditionally drawn from right to left. Start by writing a brief description of the problem in a box on the right-hand side of a whiteboard. Draw a line out to the left across the board (think of this as the head and spine of the fish – see Figure 6.2).

Then draw lines off for the major groups of factors that may affect the problem. It's helpful to use a standardized list of factors to make sure your analysis is comprehensive – for example, five Ms in manufacturing (machine, method, material, manpower, and measurement), four Ps in marketing (product, price, place, and promotion), or the McKinsey seven Ss (strategy, structure, systems, shared values, skills, style, and staff). This will give you a diagram like Figure 6.3.

For each major group of factors, brainstorm (see #48) the different elements that make up each factor and the possible causes of the problem for each. You can then evaluate each one in turn.

This process gives you a robust "map" of the problem situation, and the possible causes at every point, so you are more likely to find the real root causes than if you used a less structured approach.

Tip

Again, you'll get the best results with this technique if you do your brainstorming with a group of people who have a mixture of relevant technical expertise in the subject and direct practical experience of the problem.

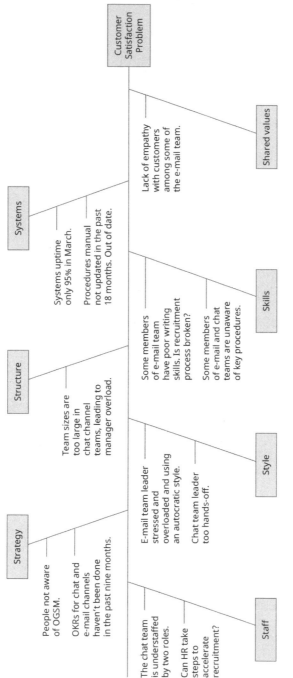

FIGURE 6.1 A Cause and Effect Diagram Highlighting a Problem within a Service Center

Strategy
- People not aware of OGSM.
- OKRs for chat and e-mail channels haven't been done in the past nine months.

Structure
- Team sizes are too large in chat channel teams, leading to manager overload.

Systems
- Systems uptime only 95% in March.
- Procedures manual not updated in the past 18 months. Out of date.

Customer Satisfaction Problem

Shared values
- Lack of empathy with customers among some of the e-mail team.

Staff
- The chat team is understaffed by two roles.
- Can HR take steps to accelerate recruitment?

Style
- E-mail team leader stressed and overloaded and using an autocratic style.
- Chat team leader too hands-off.

Skills
- Some members of e-mail team have poor writing skills. Is recruitment process broken?
- Some members of e-mail and chat teams are unaware of key procedures.

72

```
                                                          Customer
                                                          Satisfaction
                                                          Problem
```

FIGURE 6.2   The Head and Spine of the Example in Figure 6.1

Find out more about cause and effect diagrams: http://mnd.tools/34

35. Map Business Processes Clearly (Swim Lane Diagrams)

Cause and effect diagrams (#34) are great for taking a top-down view of a situation, but they don't help you think about how work is done within it. This is the domain of business process management, and many of the problems an organization experiences come from issues with its internal processes.

The first step in improving a business process is to map it out so you can fully understand the complexities of what is being done right now. As a manager, you're unlikely to be aware of many of the steps involved in delivering a high-quality product (especially when you have a highly skilled team with people who are used to taking a lot of personal responsibility).

Swim lane diagrams – developed by Geary Rummler and Alan Brache – are a useful way to map who does what and in what order. You can see an example of a swim lane diagram in Figure 6.4.

To draw a swim lane diagram, follow these steps:

1. *Define the scope of your work.* Decide which processes you want to focus on. Keep the scope of your work as narrow as you can, and be clear on what the desired output from the process is – for example, order fulfillment.
2. *List the people and groups that use the process.* List the groups of people who provide input to, work with, or receive outputs from the process.
3. *Gather a problem-solving team, including people who routinely use the process.* Bring representatives from each group.

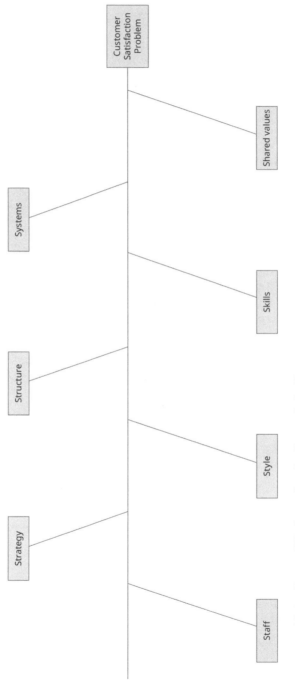

FIGURE 6.3 Major Bones Filled out for the Example in Figure 6.1

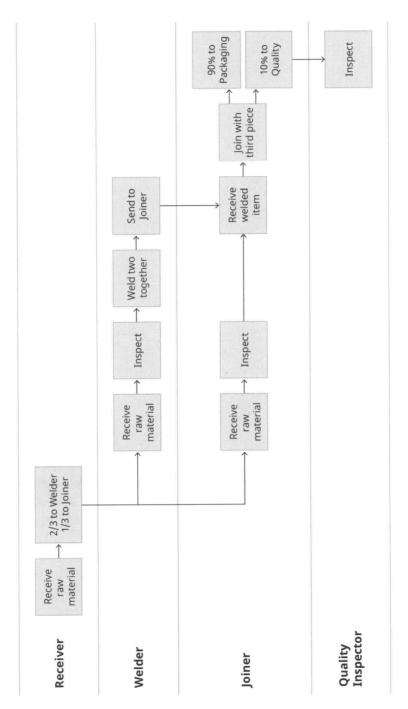

FIGURE 6.4 An Example of a Swim Lane Diagram

Make sure that these are people who actually use the process, as well as those who manage it.

4. *Set up the "swim lanes."* Draw horizontal bands across the page, and label these with the names of the groups you've identified, in the order that they're involved in the process.

5. *Map the process.* Start with the very first action in the process, whether it's receiving raw materials, placing an order, etc. Draw this as a box on the left, then map out the process as it *actually* happens, not as it should happen in a perfect world. Follow the process through sequentially, drawing boxes for each step (with the boxes being placed in the correct swim lane for the team performing the activity), and linking them with arrows.

6. *Analyze the diagram.* Once it's complete, work step-by-step through the process, and, in a blame-free way, identify either problems that people are experiencing at each stage of the process or potential points of failure where things could go wrong (these will often occur at handover points between teams). Look for steps that are missing, such as inspection points; overlaps where teams are repeating the same activity; and activities that are no longer needed or that add no value, such as creation of reports that no one reads.

7. *Remap the process as it should be.* Now draw a new swim lane diagram showing the process as it should be – with problems resolved, possible points of failure managed, and activities restructured – so that they're done as efficiently as possible. You can then do a gap analysis (#30) between the two diagrams to identify the changes that you need to make.

As an aside, this type of analysis was reinvented as *business process re-engineering* during the 1990s. For a while, it became extremely popular, only to be discredited because many companies used it as a way of justifying mass redundancies. However, the underlying notion that business processes need to be periodically reviewed and simplified is still entirely valid.

> **Tip**
>
> Be careful to run your analysis meetings in a nonhierarchical, blame-free way. Otherwise, people lower in the organization's hierarchy may be too scared to contribute.

Find out more about swim lane diagrams, and download our template for it: http://mnd.tools/35

---

36. Solve Problems by Capitalizing on What's Going Well (The 5-D Approach to Appreciative Inquiry)

We've looked at useful techniques for identifying things that are going wrong within an organization, and these are clearly very useful. However, there's also a completely different approach – appreciative inquiry – which focuses on what's going *well*. For example, imagine you're running a health club and you're struggling to retain members. In addition to focusing on solving the problems that are causing people to leave, you can ask long-term members what they love about the club. You can then work with your team to actively market these things to bring in new members who'll appreciate the things you're already doing well.

Appreciative inquiry is often conducted using a 4-D approach – discover, dream, design, and deliver. Here, we're adding in a define stage, making five Ds:

> *Define* – If you are working with a problem that needs resolving, your starting definition will probably be quite negative. So express it in a positive way: For example, if you are trying to stop members from leaving, define the goal as "to delight long-term members and thereby increase retention."

Discover – Next, look at what is going really well. In our example, you could interview long-term members and find out what they most like about the health club. Bring together their answers to identify the top factors that matter to them – let's say here that they love a particular type of exercise class that you run.

Dream – Pick up on the top factors you identified in the discover phase and brainstorm "what might be" – how you can take these positives and build on them to take them to the very best level. You might run this class more often, make the studio environment nicer, or bring in "celebrity" instructors.

Design – In this phase, you choose which of these dream ideas to work out and how.

Deliver – Implement your plan, and as you do so, make sure that you communicate these new positives to the people you serve in an inspiring, exciting way.

Enjoy using appreciative inquiry – it's an uplifting and transformational technique!

Find out more about appreciative inquiry: http://mnd.tools/36

Source: Adapted from Kessler 2013. Reproduced with permission of Sage Publications, Inc.

37. Bring People Together to Solve Problems (Manage Group Dynamics)

When we're faced with a thorny problem, our first instinct is often to gather our team to discuss it. Groups bring a diversity of perspectives to a problem, and of course their buy-in is needed to implement whatever solution is chosen. In our survey of 15,000 managers, "bringing people together to solve problems" was the most popular in the whole category of problem-solving techniques.

But there can be big practical challenges here because groups do not always function in effective or efficient ways. There are plenty of famous cases where groups have gotten into "groupthink" mode or have fallen out with each other, and have ended up making spectacularly bad decisions.

You need to understand these risks so you can guard against them. Research has identified a number of issues to watch out for:

Too much homogeneity – For example, when most of the group comes from similar professional, social, or cultural backgrounds. With little diversity of experience to draw upon, the range of solutions is likely to be narrow.

Weak leadership – Without a strong leader, more dominant members of the group – who may lack key information – can take charge, leading to a lack of direction, infighting, and a focus on the wrong priorities.

Diffusion of responsibility – Here, people can subconsciously try to share their responsibility for solving a problem with the group, meaning that no one feels accountable for the situation and the right things do not get done.

Excessive deference to authority – This is where people hold back their contrary opinions out of respect for a leader, even though they have information that shows that the direction being taken is wrong.

Evaluation apprehension – This happens when people feel that they are being judged harshly by other group members and they hold back their opinions to avoid criticism.

Free riding – Here, some group members take it easy and leave their colleagues to do the hard work, thinking that their lack of contribution will not be spotted.

Groupthink – This is where people place a desire for consensus and being part of an "in group" above their desire to reach the right decision, again narrowing the range of solutions available.

Insufficient idea development – Here, people don't fully develop each idea before they go off on a tangent to explore the next idea, and this means that they can end up selecting less than ideal solutions.

Blocking – Where bad behavior from certain individuals in a group prevents information flowing freely between members of a team. Types of blocking include *aggression* (being unhelpfully combative), *negation* (excessive criticism), *recognition-seeking* (egocentric suggestions), *withdrawing* (disengaging from the discussion), and *joking* (using humor at inappropriate times).

So how can you avoid these problems?

Start by selecting a group of people with diverse professional expertise and cultural experiences. Give them time at the start of the session to think, as individuals, about how they'd solve the problem so they can develop their own ideas in some depth. Encourage them to come up with several options so that they've thought beyond the most obvious solutions.

Then, during the session, make sure to manage the process – in other words, take stock periodically of the way the conversation is going, and be prepared to intervene if you think that group dynamics are going awry.

Discover other things you can do to avoid problems with
group dynamics: http://mnd.tools/37-1
Learn more about avoiding groupthink: http://mnd.tools/37-2

Other Useful Problem-Solving Techniques

So which useful problem-solving techniques didn't make the cut in our global survey of 15,000 businesspeople? Three are particularly useful, and you can discover them at http://mnd.tools/c6c.

Chapter 7

Make Smart Decisions

One of the great puzzles in the business world (and indeed in other walks of life such as politics) is explaining why smart people often make dumb decisions. For example, Blockbuster's executives had the opportunity to buy Netflix for $50 million in 2000, but they turned it down – and Netflix went on to wipe Blockbuster out entirely. To make sense of decisions like these, we not only need to understand the strategic context in which they were made, but we also need to consider the psychology and group dynamics of the decision makers. Although there are many benefits to getting multiple people involved in decision making, it turns out that teams are often remarkably dysfunctional.

To make better decisions as a manager, you first need to understand established techniques that provide systematic insight into the issue at hand. For the most part, these are highly rational techniques. The first is to decide if an investment or a choice makes financial sense on the basis of current information (#38). Then you need to take into account multiple quantitative and qualitative factors (#39), and a broader range of qualitative aspects such as opportunities, risks, reactions, and ethics (#40). You need to consider the downsides as well, in terms of understanding what could potentially go wrong (#41) and prioritizing risks by impact and probability of occurrence (#42).

But it is also important to be conscious of the limitations of all these techniques. In particular, you need to be aware of your own cognitive biases and flaws, so that you can avoid making the types of blunders that sometimes derail the smartest executive teams. There has been an enormous amount of research on this issue, and we suggest one framework called avoiding cognitive biases in decision making (#43) to acclimatize you to it. We also provide links to other sources of advice on this at the end of the chapter.

Needless to say, the best decision makers are adept at combining the rational and more intuition-based elements of the process: They gather all the available data to arrive at a provisional outcome, but then they allow their experience and intuition to guide them to their final decision. Amazon.com, for example, is well-known for using data to inform its decision making but also for occasionally making enormous leap-of-faith decisions, such as launching the Kindle or moving into the movie-making business.

38. Decide Whether a Decision Makes Financial Sense (Net Present Value Analysis)

The baseline for any business decision is some sort of financial projection – will this project make money? Such analyses become complex very quickly, and this is not the place to get into the details of financial analysis. But it is important to understand the basic principles and, in particular, the notion of net present value (NPV) that is central to most financial projections and spreadsheet analyses.

In crude terms, every business decision involves spending money to make money. But the timings of these cash flows – money out and money in – are vitally important because a dollar today is more valuable than a dollar tomorrow. So, how do we quantify this?

This is where NPV analysis comes in – it is a way of calculating the value of a future payment as if it were made today by applying a "discount rate." For example, $100 paid to you one year from now with a discount rate of 10% would have an NPV of $90.

NPV analysis involves estimating all the future cash flows (in and out) for a specific project under consideration and then discounting all these cash flows back to the present to figure out how profitable the project is.

For example, let's say a manager needs to decide whether to refurbish his factory's machines or buy new ones. Refurbishing (for $100,000) costs less than buying new machines (for $200,000), but buying new delivers a higher stream of cash flow. Thus, over a five-year period, we compare as follows:

Year	0	1	2	3	4	5
Refurbish	(100,000)	50,000	50,000	30,000	20,000	10,000
Buy new	(200,000)	30,000	100,000	70,000	70,000	70,000

You can see that the initial investment is paid back more quickly in the refurbish scenario – two years, rather than three. Some people like to think in these terms, but it is not advisable because it fails to account for the longer-term benefits that might accrue from the investment.

NPV analysis applies a discount rate to each of these cash flows. If you assume a discount rate of 10%, you get the results below. It suggests the manager should buy new machines because the investment delivers, over a five-year period, a higher net present value.

Year	0	1	2	3	4	5	NPV
Refurbish	(100,000)	45,455	41,322	22,539	13,660	6,209	29,186
Buy new	(200,000)	27,273	82,645	52,592	47,811	43,464	53,785
Discount Factor	1.000	0.909	0.826	0.751	0.683	0.621	

This basic calculation can be made a lot more sophisticated if you wish – you can create scenarios with different discount rates, and you can look at longer time periods. A variant of this analysis is called internal rate of return, which is a way of determining the discount rate for a given project assuming the NPV is set to zero. However, such details are beyond the scope of this book. We provide a reference below if you want to know more about this topic.

Find out more about NPVs and internal rates of return, including discovering how they are calculated: http://mnd.tools/38

39. Choose Between Options and Considering Multiple Factors (Decision Matrix Analysis)

Few decisions in business come down to just a single factor, such as cost. For example, if you choose a supplier purely because they offer the lowest price, you can end up with poor-quality goods, or you may find the goods are produced in an unethical way, such as using child labor.

So you need to take many different factors into account in your decision making, and this can feel like comparing apples to oranges. How do you do this in a rigorous way that you can justify to people who may later challenge your decision? This is where decision matrix analysis can help.

1. List the factors you want to use to make your decision as column headings in a table, similar to Figure 7.1.

2. Enter a row on the table for numerical weightings that you'll apply to each factor. These show its relative importance, measured on a scale of, say, 1 to 5. If one of your factors is relatively unimportant, give it a 1; if it's highly important, give it a 5. You can see an example in Figure 7.2: Cost and quality are highly important in the final decision, but the supplier's location and delivery reliability don't matter as much – perhaps there are plenty of quick alternatives if delivery fails.

Factors	Cost	Quality	Location	Reliability	Payment Options	Total

Figure 7.1   Column Headings Showing Decision Factors

Factors	Cost	Quality	Location	Reliability	Payment Options	Total
Weights	4	5	1	2	3	

Figure 7.2   Applying a Weighting to Each Decision Factor

Factors	Cost	Quality	Location	Reliability	Payment Options	Total
Weights	4	5	1	2	3	
Supplier 1	1	0	0	1	3	
Supplier 2	0	3	2	2	1	
Supplier 3	2	2	1	3	0	
Supplier 4	2	3	3	3	0	

FIGURE 7.3   Adding Options and Scoring These by Each Factor

Factors	Cost	Quality	Location	Reliability	Payment Options	Total
Weights	4	5	1	2	3	
Supplier 1	4	0	0	2	9	15
Supplier 2	0	15	2	4	3	24
Supplier 3	8	10	1	6	0	25
Supplier 4	8	15	3	6	0	32

FIGURE 7.4   Weighting Each Score and Calculating the Total

3. Enter table rows underneath for each of the options you're evaluating. For each row, score the option by each factor on a scale of 0 to 5, where 0 means that the option is very poor and 5 means that it's very good. (Ignore weightings at this stage.) See Figure 7.3.

4. Finally, multiply each of these scores by the weighting for each factor, and total each row. This shows how well each option scores relative to the other options, and answers the question of which option is best for you. You can see this in Figure 7.4. (Here, the row values shown are the scores from step 3 multiplied by the weighting from step 2. In this example, supplier 4 is the best option because it offers the best mix of quality, location, and reliability of delivery.)

Tips

◆ As you're doing this, be aware that some things may cause you to completely reject one of your options—for example, if they pose a risk to team members' health or safety or if they involve activities that contravene the ethical code of your organization. Where this happens, you need to consider ruling the entire option out.

◆ Always use your intuition to check your answer. If your intuition is telling you you've ended up with the wrong result, check your assumptions carefully.

Find out more about decision matrix analysis, and download a decision matrix analysis template: http://mnd.tools/39

40. Consider Many Factors, Such as Opportunities, Risks, Reactions, and Ethics in Decision Making (ORAPAPA)

NPV and decision matrix analyses help you choose between options in quite a robust way. However, there are many reasons why they don't give you the full picture, so it is always important to sense-check your decision. This is particularly important given the cognitive biases and flawed group dynamics that often plague decision making (as we discuss in #43). Although you can never entirely prevent flawed thinking, you can at least become more conscious of the potential risks you are facing.

This is where the ORAPAPA checklist comes in handy as a list of factors to consider when you're evaluating a significant decision. It's particularly useful for teams, because it allows people to step back from entrenched positions they may naturally adopt and helps them look at the decision using a variety of perspectives that they may not intuitively use.

ORAPAPA stands for opportunities, risks, alternatives and improvements, past experience, analysis, people, and alignment and ethics. Take a course of action you're looking at, and sense-check it using each heading:

Opportunities – By brainstorming the opportunities the decision opens up, the team can bring the positives out into the open. This ensures that the optimists on your team are fairly heard and that their opinions are respected.

Risks – With all of the enthusiasm and passion that goes into making a case for change, it's easy to underplay the risks that can go along with a decision. So this heading gives your team permission to explore the risks thoroughly without being labeled "naysayers." Considering risk properly is a fundamentally important part of making mature, wise decisions as we discuss in more depth in #41.

Alternatives and improvements – It takes a lot of effort to reach agreement on a particular option. Even then, there may be problems with that option, including foreseeable negative consequences and risks that you need to address. So are there further alternatives you should consider? And could you improve the idea still further?

Past experience –Your organization may have tried something similar before. Situations change, and what may not have worked in the past may work now, but it's foolish not to learn from past experience. So spend time thinking about similar situations in the past and how you can learn from them.

Analysis – Check the numbers used to support your decision, and make sure that these are robust. Ensure that sufficient analysis has been done, and double-check any explicit or unknowing assumptions you may have made. Then ask yourself whether your decision is aligned with general trends in the market, and sense-check your decision-making process to ensure that it hasn't been affected by issues of poor group dynamics (see #37) or psychological bias (see #43).

People – Think about how your stakeholders and the wider community will react to the decision based on their limited knowledge (remember, most people will have no appetite for understanding the detailed pros and cons of your decision – they will use their intuition or "gut" to tell them whether they agree with it). This step prompts you to ensure that you've thought about stakeholder management and stakeholder communication – see Chapter 18 for more on this.

Alignment and ethics – Finally, you need to confirm that the decision aligns with your organization's vision and mission and that it is ethical. This is tricky if you stand to make a lot of money, or if you're heavily emotionally invested because of all the work you've done on the decision. However, as we've seen in all sorts of recent, high-profile cases, ethical lapses can be disastrous for organizations and for the individuals involved.

Find out more about ORAPAPA: http://mnd.tools/40

41. Analyze Systematically What Could Go Wrong (Risk Analysis and Risk Management)

As we saw in #40, risk is something we always need to consider when we're making a significant decision. Almost all business decisions involve risk of some kind and the possibility of damage being done to the organization.

The trick is not to avoid risk altogether but rather to identify and understand the risks you're engaging with and manage them in an appropriate, pragmatic way. Openness to a balanced risk analysis is, therefore, a key differentiator between being seen as an unreliable "loose cannon" or a trustworthy and wise leader.

There are two parts to risk – the scale of a possible negative consequence (often measured as a cost) and the likelihood of it happening (measured as a probability). The first part of risk analysis is to identify possible threats. For big decisions, it's useful to gather together an experienced, multidisciplinary team to provide a range of insights into the range of threats you might face.

In a stable, established industry, you may be able to draw on established risk management protocols or checklists to give your team a good starting point for assessing risk. But it's still useful to supplement these with a mixture of failure mode and effects analysis (FMEA) (see the URL below), a cause and effect analysis-like approach (#34), and brainstorming (#48) to try to spot other risks that are specific to your situation.

If you're in a less established business setting, you'll need to use a range of approaches and develop your own framework. The range of risk areas is likely to be much broader – for example, including human, operational, reputational, procedural, financial, technical, natural, and political risks – see the URL for this below.

The next step is to estimate the risk. For each risk factor, estimate the cost if it occurs (usually relatively straightforward) and the probability of it occurring (typically much harder). By multiplying cost and probability together, you can get a value for each risk, and this can help you prioritize. (See #42 for more on this.)

How can you manage the risks you've identified? Review the most important ones, and think about how you can avoid them, mitigate them to a reasonable level, or transfer them – for example, by paying for insurance or hedging a currency transaction. Ultimately, there will be some risks that you need to accept, and you'll need to create contingency plans to manage them if they occur. (For more on risk management, follow the link below.)

Tips

- ◆ As we said earlier in this chapter, you need to think particularly carefully where risks affect people's health and safety or the survival of your organization.
- ◆ Just as you need to listen to your intuition when choosing between options, you need to listen to it when you're analyzing risks. You'll make your best choices when you use both intuition and rationality!

Find out more about risk analysis and risk management:	http://mnd.tools/41-1
Find out more about FMEA:	http://mnd.tools/41-2
Discover how to conduct contingency planning:	http://mnd.tools/41-3

42. Prioritize Risks by Impact and Probability of Occurrence (The Risk Impact/Probability Chart)

Risk analysis is important, but you can quickly end up with a worryingly long list of possible risks. It can be intensely time-consuming to address all of them, and this is where the risk impact/probability chart comes in (see Figure 7.5) as a way of identifying the ones you should focus most of your effort on.

An approach that has been in general use for several decades, the chart suggests four generic categories of risks:

Low impact/low probability risks – These risks are unlikely to materialize, and it doesn't matter much if they do. You can often ignore them and just cope with negative consequences as they appear.

Low impact/high probability risks – You can cope with these if they occur, but you should take sensible steps to stop them from happening because they can slow you down.

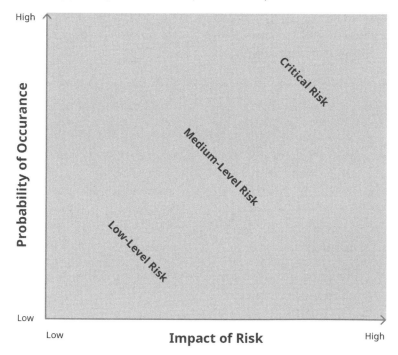

FIGURE 7.5   **Risk Impact/Probability Chart**

High impact/low probability – These are unlikely to occur but can cause big problems if they do. Do what you sensibly can to reduce the impact if they transpire, and make sure you have appropriate contingency plans to deal with them. Pay particular attention to risks involving people's lives or the failure of your organization; for everyone's sake, you need to protect against these situations carefully.

High impact/high probability – These risks are of key importance, and you need to focus large amounts of your time and resources on managing them.

Tip

Although we can identify four categories of risks here, we specifically *don't* show this chart as a 2 × 2 matrix. It is more useful to think in terms of diagonal slices where the risks in the top-right are most critical and those in the bottom-left are least critical.

Find out more about risk impact/probability charts,
including downloading a template for drawing them: http://mnd.tools/42

---

43. Avoid Psychological Bias in Decision Making

Imagine you're researching a potential product. You think the market is growing, and as part of your research you find information that supports this belief. As a result, you launch the product, backed by a major marketing campaign, but the product fails. The market hasn't expanded, so there are fewer customers than you expected. You can't sell enough of your products to cover their costs, and you end up with a loss.

In this scenario, your decision was affected by confirmation bias. You interpreted market information in a way that confirmed your preconceptions – instead of seeing it objectively – and you made the wrong decision as a result.

Confirmation bias is one of many psychological biases to which we're all susceptible when we make decisions. There is now an enormous body of thinking about this phenomenon, building on the work of the Nobel Prize – winning psychologist Daniel Kahneman and his late collaborator Amos Tversky.

Psychological bias – also known as cognitive bias – is the tendency to make decisions or take actions that go against systematic logic. For example, you might subconsciously make selective use of data, or you might feel pressured to make a decision by powerful colleagues. Psychological bias is the opposite of clear, measured judgment. It can lead to missed opportunities and poor decision making. Here are five common psychological biases that can lead us to make poor business decisions.

1. CONFIRMATION BIAS

As in the earlier example, confirmation bias happens when you subconsciously look for information that supports your existing beliefs. This can lead you to make biased decisions because you don't factor in all relevant information.

To avoid confirmation bias, look for ways to challenge what you think you see. Seek out information from a range of sources, and use an approach such as ORAPAPA (#40) to consider situations from multiple perspectives. Alternatively, discuss your thoughts with others: Surround yourself with a diverse group of people, and don't be afraid to listen to dissenting views.

2. ANCHORING

This is the tendency to base your final judgment on information gained early in the decision-making process. For example, when negotiating on price, the initial figure suggested, even if it seems ridiculously high, will often shape the price you end up paying. Think of this as a first impression bias. Once you form an initial picture of a situation, it's hard to see other possibilities.

To overcome the risk of anchoring affecting your judgment, reflect on your decision-making history, and think about whether you've rushed to judgment in the past. Often it is a good idea to ask for more time if you feel pressured to make a quick decision. (If someone is pressing aggressively for a decision, this can be a sign they're pushing against your best interests.)

3. OVERCONFIDENCE BIAS

This occurs when you place too much faith in your own knowledge and opinions. You may believe that your contribution to a decision is more valuable than it actually is. You might combine this bias with anchoring, meaning that you act on hunches, because you have an unrealistic view of your own decision-making ability.

To overcome this bias, consider the sources of information you tend to rely on when you make decisions: Are they fact-based, or do you rely on hunches? And to what extent are you relying on your prior successes as a source of insight rather than factoring in failures? If you suspect that you might be depending on potentially unreliable information, try to gather more objective data.

4. GAMBLER'S FALLACY

With the gambler's fallacy, you expect past events to influence the future. A classic example is a coin toss: If you get heads seven times consecutively, you might assume that there's a higher chance that you'll toss tails the eighth time; and the longer the run, the stronger your belief may be that things will change the next time. Of course, the odds are always 50/50.

The gambler's fallacy can be dangerous in a business environment. Imagine you're an investment analyst in a highly volatile market. Your four previous investments did well, and you plan to make a new, much larger one because you see a pattern of success. In fact, outcomes are highly uncertain, and the number of successes that you've had previously has only a small bearing on the future.

To avoid the gambler's fallacy, make sure that you look at trends from a number of angles. Drill deep into data, and try to develop a realistic view of future odds. If you notice patterns in behavior or product success – for example, if several projects fail unexpectedly – look for trends in your environment, such as changed customer preferences or wider economic circumstances.

5. FUNDAMENTAL ATTRIBUTION ERROR

This is the tendency to blame others when things go wrong instead of looking objectively at the situation. In particular, you may blame or judge someone based on a stereotype or a perceived personality flaw.

For example, if you're in a car accident and the other driver is at fault, you're more likely to assume that he or she is a bad driver than you are to consider whether bad weather played a role. However, if *you* have a car accident that's your fault, you're more likely to blame the brakes or the wet road than your reaction time.

To avoid this error, it's essential to look at situations, and the people involved in them, nonjudgmentally. Use empathy to understand why people behave in the ways they do and build emotional intelligence so that you can reflect accurately on your own behavior.

Note

It's hard to spot psychological bias in ourselves because it often comes from subconscious thinking. For this reason, it can be unwise to make major decisions on your own, without discussing them with other people.

Learn more about avoiding psychological bias: http://mnd.tools/43

Other Useful Decision-Making Techniques

In addition to the tools recommended in our survey, we believe that you need to use a robust process to make good decisions, and you need to conclude this with a solid go/no-go decision. Find out more about these at http://mnd.tools/c7c.

Chapter 8

Foster Creativity and Innovation

As a manager, you are always looking for ways to improve performance – for example, by making your products and services more attractive or by increasing internal efficiency. Many of the tools we discussed in previous chapters help you do this – they are ways of generating continuous improvements within an established framework. But sometimes you need or have an opportunity to move into uncharted territory – to innovate. This might mean creating a new product or service that hasn't been seen before, or it might mean trying out radically different ways of working.

This chapter introduces a range of tools that help you with creativity and innovation. For many managers, this is uncomfortable territory because, by definition, innovation means trying something new and accepting the risk that it may not work out. And there is often a feeling that innovation is someone else's job – the R&D department or the business development team.

Our view is that all managers can be creative and innovative and that they need to encourage people in their teams to be so as well. But we know this isn't easy. You need to develop strong social and political skills to sell your innovative ideas to others in the organization, a topic we address in Chapters 16 and 17. And you need frameworks and stimuli to help you think outside of the box – to come up with creative ideas that you can then explore in detail. That is what this chapter is all about.

The first two techniques we look at are about trying to see the world through the eyes of your customers rather than assuming you already know what they need. Design thinking (#44) is a very popular way of coming up with business ideas from a user's perspective and developing them through a process of rapid prototyping. Ethnography (#45) is a very specific technique, often used as part of design thinking, for tapping into the unarticulated needs of prospective customers.

In addition to gaining inspiration from customers, it is also useful to gain inspiration from the future, and that is where scenario planning (#46) comes in. We also suggest two other techniques – Doblin's 10 types of innovation (#47), which helps you think broadly about the different forms of innovation open to you, and brainstorming (#48), which is a tried-and-tested way of generating ideas around a particular theme through a group process.

44. Develop New Ideas by Understanding User Needs (Design Thinking)

Traditionally, many companies approach product development through technological innovation – they work on what is technically feasible in an R&D laboratory, and they get designers and marketers involved in the latter stages of the process to help make the product more visually appealing, or to position it in an attractive way.

Although this approach isn't wrong, it has significant limitations. It is very common for R&D people to work on technologically interesting problems, regardless of whether they have any value in the marketplace; this technology-centered approach often results in over-engineered or ill-conceived products. Famous examples include the Segway, Nokia's N-Gage, and the Apple Newton.

In today's competitive markets, a more thoughtful approach to innovation is required. Clearly, there are many industries where technological development is important, but more than that, it is vital to have a deep understanding of user needs.

In most business-to-consumer (B2C) markets, customers search out end-user ratings and product reviews online and use them to choose between the many options available to them. In these cases, underlying technologies are often relatively unimportant because many organizations can master them and integrate them well. What really matters is how the product meets a customer's practical and emotional needs. For this to happen, the development process needs to be driven by a deep understanding of customer needs right from the start.

This is where an approach called design thinking is useful. Pioneered as early as 1969, and more recently championed by the California design agency IDEO, the design thinking process can be simplified to the key steps shown in Figure 8.1.

The high-level steps in this process are:

1. *Understand the business problem and constraints.* Here, you need to develop a clear understanding of the problem you're trying to solve. This isn't always as obvious as it seems. For example, if you work for a university and you are getting feedback that the lectures are poor, you might conclude that the problem is either poor-quality lecturers who need training or lecture rooms that are badly designed and need a refit. However, a design-led approach to this problem would be to look at the bigger picture and ask what the purpose of the lectures is in the first place. This might reorient the analysis toward providing students with a high-quality education. At this stage, you also need to consider the resources you have available and the constraints you're operating under. This defines the context of the rest of the process.

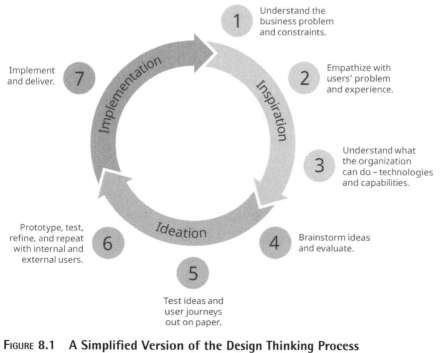

FIGURE 8.1 A Simplified Version of the Design Thinking Process

Source: Brown 2008. Reproduced with permission of Harvard Business Publishing.

2. *Empathize with users' problem and experience.* Next, you need to talk to and understand your target customers, appreciate how they see the world, empathize with their life situation and experience, and understand what they want, like, and engage with. (We look at this in more depth in #45.)

3. *Understand what the organization can do – technologies and capabilities.* This involves exploring what the organization is capable of doing well and what it won't be able to do.

4. *Brainstorm ideas and evaluate.* Having understood the context, brainstorm ideas (#48). Then evaluate them and select the most promising ones.

5. *Test ideas and user journeys out on paper.* For promising ideas, draft them on paper and put yourself into the mind of your users. Think about what their experience will be, both with the product you're thinking of and with competing products.

6. *Prototype, test, refine, and repeat with internal and external users.* Take the best ideas forward and build prototypes of them. Test these with users, and go through repeated cycles of refinement until you are confident they would buy them.

7. *Implement and deliver.* Now take your best-received prototype through to production.

Clearly, this is a longer, more time-consuming way of developing a new product than the traditional approach, but it is one that is much more likely to deliver a solution that customers love.

Find out more about design thinking here: http://mnd.tools/44

---

45. Innovate by Studying People's Day-to-Day Use of Products and Services in Depth (Ethnographic Research)

The second step in design thinking (#44) is about understanding users' experience, and this is where ethnographic research is particularly useful. Rather than asking your customers what they think of your product, ethnographic research is about observing *how* they use it in order to pick up hints about how you might improve your offering. It is about tapping into unarticulated needs.

Ethnography started off as a branch of anthropology, focusing on studying people as they live their everyday lives. In recent decades, it has been used in business. Companies like Intel® have conducted ethnographic studies to understand long-term trends in the use and application of technology, whereas others like Procter & Gamble have used this method to understand people's day-to-day living habits. For example, the best-selling Swiffer, which uses a disposable cloth rather than a wet mop to clean floors, emerged from a lengthy ethnographic study of home-cleaning behavior.

There are a variety of ways that you can conduct ethnographic research to improve the way you serve customers. One is to shadow the consumers you're studying – watch how they behave, talk to them about what they're thinking, and learn from this. This can involve just watching them in a specific location, or it can even mean moving in with them for a short period of time to watch their lives and fully understand their thoughts and behaviors.

Other approaches involve incentivizing customers to track their experience of situations or brands with journals or smartphone apps. Or it could be getting them to conduct short "missions" you give them and record what they're thinking as they complete them. Meanwhile, there are many website plugins you can use to record how people interact with online services and many user testing services that allow paid testers to record their thoughts.

Ethnographic research can be prone to biases, such as customers thinking more about their decisions than they normally would or changing their behavior to please you. It is also very time-consuming, so you need to commit a significant amount of time and resources to get the best from this type of research. But as a way of gaining new insights into the unstated needs of your customers, it is well worth the effort.

Learn more about ethnographic research: http://mnd.tools/45

46. Innovate by Making Sense of How the Business World Is Changing (Scenario Planning)

Design thinking and ethnographic research are great techniques for innovating around the needs of users, as those needs exist today. A very different approach to innovation is to look at how the world is changing and to position your business accordingly. As ice hockey legend Wayne Gretzky said, "I don't skate to where the puck is – I skate to where the puck is going to be."

How do you develop the right products and services for a fast-changing business world? This is where scenario planning, as shown in Figure 8.2, is useful. It is a method of thinking in a structured way about how the future might look so that you can create a small number of scenarios that reflect the most likely

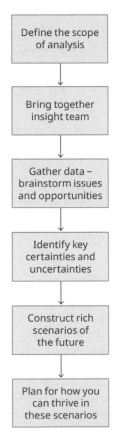

FIGURE **8.2 The Scenario Planning Process**

Source: Adapted from Schwartz 1991. Reproduced with permission of John Wiley & Sons, Inc.

and significant outcomes. You can then design products and services that best fit these new circumstances. Use the following steps:

1. *Define the scope of your analysis,* particularly the time horizon that you want to consider, and the business areas you want to focus on.

2. *Bring together a team of people with insight into the future.* These might be experts in your industry or in key technology areas, customers or people affected by your work, people who have developed economic forecasts covering the period, and so on.

3. *Gather data, and brainstorm trends, issues, risks, and opportunities.* Concentrate on exploring and listing as many of these as you can, perhaps using a framework such as PESTLIED (political–economic–sociocultural–technological–legal–international–environmental–demographic) analysis (#82) to help.

4. *Identify key certainties and uncertainties.* Separate out things that are very likely to happen from things that will matter a lot to you that you cannot predict one way or another. For example, if you work for an insurance company, an aging population is a certainty, whereas future crime rates or the rollout of driverless automobiles are uncertainties. Group these together into closely related themes, and then rank the certainties and uncertainties separately, in order of their importance to you and their likeliness to come about.

5. *Construct rich scenarios of the future.* Using the certainties and uncertainties you've identified, construct a small number of detailed scenarios of how the future will look over the time horizon you've identified. The certainties you've identified will apply to all of these, while the scenarios should explore the most likely possible outcomes of the most important uncertainties.

6. *Think about how your organization can thrive in each of these scenarios.* For each one, think about how your organization will need to change to flourish in it and what products and services you will need to offer to manage risk and be successful.

The opportunities for innovation exist in the final stage: You need to think about how these scenarios might affect demand for your products and services, or how entirely new offerings might emerge if these scenarios come to pass. Depending on what you come up with, you might need to do some additional research or development work to develop your ideas further.

Tips

◆ It can take a lot of work to construct, discuss, and examine scenarios, and if you create too many of them, you risk not examining any of them in enough depth. Try to keep to three to five scenarios only.

◆ Peter Schwartz, one of the originators of scenario analysis, suggests four ways that trends can evolve over time:

Evolution: All trends continue as expected, in a predictable direction.

Revolution: A new factor fundamentally changes the situation.

Cycles: Boom follows bust follows boom follows bust.

Infinite expansion: Exciting trends continue indefinitely.

Find out more about scenario analysis here, including seeing a worked example of the process in action: http://mnd.tools/46

47. Innovate in All Areas of Your Business, Not Just with Products and Services (Doblin's 10 Types of Innovation)

When we think about fostering creativity and innovation, it's very easy to focus on product or service innovation only – after all, this is what our customers see. However, organizations can innovate in all sorts of ways, and some of the less obvious forms of innovation are actually the most powerful.

The consulting group Doblin categorized these different types of innovation in its 2013 book *Ten Types of Innovation: The Discipline of Building Breakthroughs*. This list provides a handy way of thinking about the types of innovation that can help you build competitive advantage:

1. *Profit model innovation* – This focuses on how you generate a profit margin from your products and services – for example, using different pricing models for different customer segments, charging on a per-use basis, offering products on subscriptions, bundling services with products, etc.

2. *Network innovation* – This looks at how your business deals with its suppliers and business partners. It may involve developing highly efficient, low-cost, or resilient supply chains; building high-value strategic alliances; or bringing in specialized suppliers with specific expertise.

3. *Structure innovation* – This focuses on the structure of the organization and how its assets help create value – for example, it includes innovations that help you get the best from your people or that enable teams to work faster and more flexibly.

4. *Process innovation* – This emphasizes how you deliver products and services in an efficient, high-quality way. Six Sigma and *kaizen* are examples of methodologies for managing process innovation.

5. *Product performance innovation* – This is what people usually think about when you talk about innovation – improvements that make your products more appealing to your customers.

6. *Product system innovation* – This looks at the "offer" that goes with your product – for example, how you bundle it, package it, or customize it to sell it at a premium.

7. *Service innovation* – There are many ways to provide value-added services on top of physical products (for example, the warranties, insurance, and financing sold when you purchase an auto), and these are often more profitable than the underlying product.

8. *Channel innovation* – This focuses on expanding the routes to market – for example, selling to customers directly or online rather than through a retailer.

9. *Brand innovation* – This involves looking for ways to enhance customer perception of your brand – for example, by communicating the value of your product or service in a novel way.

10. *Customer experience innovation* – This is all about improving the experience that customers have when they interact with you and the way that they think or feel about you and your offering as they do so.

The value of this list is that it helps you to think more systematically about your options. Some of these approaches will be dead ends, but others may provide the spark of insight that helps you do something really creative.

Find out more about Doblin's 10 types of innovation here, including learning about tools that can help you with each one:　　http://mnd.tools/47

Source: Adapted from Keeley et al. 2013.

48. Generate Many Ideas Using Free Association (Brainstorming)

So far, we've looked at large-scale approaches to innovation, and these have an important place in how organizations innovate. However, teams also innovate on a smaller scale, and much of this is done through brainstorming.

Managed well, brainstorming is a highly effective tool for generating and developing ideas as a team. It can deliver exciting ideas individuals are unlikely to come up with on their own, and at the same time, it helps the team bond and move forward with everyone feeling like they've played a part.

But when run poorly, brainstorming sessions are unhappy affairs that sow division and fail to achieve any worthwhile outputs. You need to set them up with care and manage them in a way that eliminates the problems that come with poor group dynamics (#37).

It is important to understand the difference between individual brainstorming and group brainstorming. Individuals brainstorming on their own often produce a wider range of ideas than groups, whereas groups often develop ideas in a richer way. You usually get the best results by combining the two. Here is a step-by-step guide:

1. *Bring together a team with diverse but relevant experience.* You want a wide range of knowledge and experience to draw on during the brainstorming session. And you need open-minded people who are willing contributors.

2. *Present the problem, and define the ground rules.* Define the problem you want to solve, and explain the format of the meeting. In particular, make it clear that there should be no criticism of ideas, "wild" ideas will be welcomed, and everyone is expected to contribute.

3. *Give people time to come up with ideas on their own.* This ensures a good level of diversity in terms of "raw" ideas and helps people develop confidence in them. If you leap straight to group discussion, you risk getting "stuck in a rut" by fixating on a small set of ideas.

4. *Get everyone to share their ideas, and then start the discussion.* Encourage people to share ideas generously. Pay careful attention to what others are saying, and get people to build on one another's ideas by using their personal knowledge and experiences.

5. *Guide the meeting to develop plenty of ideas.* Spend long enough on each idea to develop it; then quickly move on to the next. As you're doing this, keep an eye out for any problems of poor group dynamics – these can seriously undermine a healthy brainstorming process.

6. *Bring ideas together at the end of the session.* You can use affinity diagrams (see the link below) to organize ideas into common themes. Then bring judgment back into the process, and use appropriate decision-making techniques to choose between them. (You may want to do this in a separate session to preserve the upbeat mood of a successful brainstorming session.)

Find out more about brainstorming here, along with learning about different types of brainstorming that can help you in specific situations:	http://mnd.tools/48-1
Learn how to use affinity diagrams to group information into common themes:	http://mnd.tools/48-2

Other Techniques for Fostering Creativity and Innovation

There are two important innovation processes that didn't make the cut in our survey: The Stage-Gate® idea-to-launch process and Eric Ries's build-measure-learn process. It's important to know about these; you can find out more at http://mnd.tools/c8c.

Part III

Work with and Manage Other People

Chapter 9

Understand and Motivate Other People

An increasingly popular way of defining management is "enabling people to do their best work." According to this worldview, a good boss is someone who creates a work environment where people feel highly motivated and contribute to the best of their ability.

How do you create this type of positive, high-energy work environment? The starting point is to put yourself in the shoes of your employees – so that you can understand their fears and concerns, their interests and needs. Most people want to do a good job in the workplace, and to a large extent, your role as their boss is to take obstacles out of the way and give them the space they need. Of course, as a boss, you also have to manage poor performance and bad behavior, but managing these types of difficult situations is the focus of a later chapter. In this chapter, we emphasize the positive – and even inspiring – ways you can help your people to do their best work.

Unfortunately, it's quite hard to create this type of positive working environment. Managers often find it difficult to get their team members to open up about their challenges and concerns. Often, they are so overwhelmed with tasks and with trying to keep their own bosses happy that they struggle to give their own people the attention they need. Another mistake is to adopt a "one-size-fits-all" approach to managing people, which works well for some but not for others.

This chapter provides several techniques and frameworks that help you overcome these challenges, so that you can understand your employees better and create an environment where they can do their best work.

We start with two specific techniques. Leading by example, also known as role modeling (#49), is a way of consciously exhibiting the behaviors and actions that you would like others to adopt. Mindful listening (#50) is a technique to help you make the most of discussions with people in your team – so that you properly understand what they are saying and respond in a thoughtful way.

Then we describe techniques designed to help you understand others better. First, we look at individual motivation. This is a large and complex topic, which we can only scratch the surface of here. We describe one classic framework, Herzberg's motivation-hygiene theory (#51), which provides practical insights into the things that motivate, and demotivate, your employees, and we provide references to several other approaches to motivation you might find useful. We also consider different generational characteristics (#52) to help you understand why generation Y employees (people born after 1980) have such different expectations and demands in the workplace than generation X and baby boomers.

Finally, we describe two broader frameworks that cut across these specific techniques. One is the notion of emotional intelligence (#53), which is an individual's capacity to make sense of and respond effectively to whatever is happening in his or her social environment. Emotional intelligence is a good thing for anyone to have, but it is particularly useful for someone who is trying to manage others. The other is the concept of transformational leadership (#54), which is an umbrella concept for how leaders inspire and help their employees to grow.

49. Lead by Example (Being a Good Role Model)

It is useful to start by looking at ourselves when we want to motivate and inspire others because the way we behave directly influences how others behave. "Do as I say, not do as I do" might have been acceptable to earlier generations, but it is likely to breed cynicism in today's business world.

The key idea here is that in a social environment, such as a workplace, people want to fit in, so they act in ways that seem to work for those around them (this is called social learning). Sure, we learn by being taught, by listening, and through trial and error, but we also learn by watching what other people do, seeing what does and doesn't work, and changing our behavior accordingly.

If we see people we respect stand firm and win in situations where we might usually feel scared, we learn that we can win in these situations. If we see people do things that harm others, directly or indirectly, and we see this "backfire" on them, we learn to not do these things. If we see people being rewarded for certain behaviors – even if these behaviors are bad – we learn that we may be rewarded for doing these things too, and we may do them ourselves.

This is why it's so important for us, as managers, to be good role models for the people who report to us, and it's also why we need to be careful about the behaviors we reward, whether intentionally or accidentally.

A few simple examples: If we want people to be punctual, we first need to be punctual ourselves. If we then compliment those who turn up early for meetings or we comment on people being late, people quickly get the message, and the majority will adapt accordingly. Sometimes you'll have a few holdouts – people who perhaps think they are so important they can show up late. You mustn't let them get away with this – you need to have a quiet word with these people, perhaps by reminding them that they are role models and need to act accordingly.

Equally, if we want integrity, we need to act with integrity. If we want people to control costs, we need to control our own costs. Other than explicit, contracted benefits, we shouldn't expect there to be special privileges of rank that allow us to behave differently from the people who work for us – if we want our people to do things, we need to do them ourselves.

As a manager of others, there are many levers we have at our disposal to push people to do things differently – we can change their job descriptions, we can use incentives, we can provide feedback during performance reviews, and so on. But these are heavy-handed techniques. It's always better to start by simply modeling the type of behavior we are looking for, as captured in the exhortation often attributed to Mahatma Gandhi: "Be the change you wish to see in the world."

Find out more about being an effective role model: http://mnd.tools/49

---

50. Listen Carefully and Intensely to Other People (Mindful Listening)

Being a good listener is an important life skill – it helps us boost our personal relationships, and it makes us good company. It is also a vital component of being a good boss. Indeed, when you hear people reflecting on the good and bad bosses they have had over the years, a common criticism of the bad bosses is "she was a really bad listener" or "he was only interested in his own point of view."

Listening helps us understand what upsets the people who work for us so that we can help clear these things away, and it helps us appreciate what excites and energizes them about their work so that we can help them shape their work in this direction. But how, in the hurly-burly of a busy working day, can we find time to do this, particularly if we're feeling stressed and under pressure to deliver results and if we have a hundred things on our mind?

First, you need to create opportunities to talk and listen, and this just won't happen unless you do it in a structured way. This is a key reason why it's so important to have weekly or biweekly one-on-ones with the individuals who report to you. It's pretty much impossible to be an effective manager if you are not running these. (See the URL below for more on running effective one-on-one meetings. If you are not having such meetings, stop reading and set them up right now!)

Then you need to listen carefully. You may have heard of active listening – this is about paying attention to the other person, using good body language to encourage them to talk, reflecting back what they're saying to show you're listening, deferring judgment, and responding appropriately. This is good stuff, but it's all too easy to "go through the motions" with this and *still not actually listen.*

This is where the notion of mindful listening is useful. It ensures that you are fully mentally present during the conversation and that you have put aside all other distractions so you can concentrate completely on the other person. To do this:

◆ Take a few minutes before you meet to calm yourself, clear your mind of other issues, and prepare yourself properly for the conversation.

◆ Hold it in a quiet, calm place, and mute your mobile devices so that they don't distract you.

◆ Focus completely on what the other person is saying. Concentrate on their message and their body language, and empathize with the feelings and emotions that they're expressing.

◆ Note down key points, plus any thoughts you have, so that you're not tempted to try to hold these in your mind. Do not prepare your answers to the points made.

◆ As you're listening, also pay attention to your own emotions and note these down. Then let these go, and continue to focus on the other person.

Only once the person you're talking to has finished should you pick up your notes and address the points he or she made.

Find out more about active listening:	http://mnd.tools/50-1
Learn more about mindful listening:	http://mnd.tools/50-2
Find out how to run an effective one-on-one:	http://mnd.tools/50-3

51. Understand How to Motivate People (Herzberg's Motivation-Hygiene Theory)

Although techniques such as role modeling and mindful listening are important, it is even more important to know what motivates your people. To do this, you need a solid understanding of the principles of human motivation.

There is a vast amount of research on motivation – it could be the subject of this entire book. In the interest of space, we focus on one classic approach, Frederick Herzberg's motivation-hygiene theory because it offers immediate, practical advice, especially in situations where morale is low. We also provide links below to several other important ideas and frameworks, such as Abraham Maslow's hierarchy, theories X and Y, and Sirota's three-factor theory.

Herzberg observed that the things that make people dissatisfied with their jobs (hygiene factors) are *not* the same things that make them happy with them (motivators). For example, people will be demotivated if they feel that they are being paid below the fair rate for their job, but paying them well above the market rate is likely to have only a limited or short-term motivational impact. Figure 9.1 shows Herzberg's factors for dissatisfaction and satisfaction.

So how do you use this model? The answer is to talk to your team members about themselves and how their work is going. If morale is poor and people seem unmotivated, listen particularly for the things that are making them unhappy. Ask appropriate questions to find out more, and then deal with these issues – there's no point trying to motivate and energize anyone until you've done this. Once you have, you can work on the positive motivators – for example, the way work is done and how jobs are designed.

Sure, it takes a lot of time to do these things, but using Herzberg's theory is one of the most important things you can do to transform unhappy, poorly functioning teams into enthusiastic, high-achieving ones.

Factors for Dissatisfaction	Factors for Satisfaction
Restrictive company policies	Opportunities for achievement
Bad management	Recognition
Poor relationship with supervisor and peers	The work itself
Unsatisfactory work conditions	Responsibility
Uncompetitive salary	Advancement
Low status	Personal growth
Lack of job security	

FIGURE 9.1 **Frederick Herzberg's Factors for Dissatisfaction and Satisfaction**
Source: Herzberg 1968. Reproduced with permission of Harvard Business Publishing.

> **Tip**
>
> What motivates one person can be very different from what motivates someone else. This is why it's so important to get to know your people. That way, you can deal with issues that are upsetting them and help them shape their work so that it fits with what inspires them. Regular one-on-ones really do matter!

Learn more about Herzberg's motivation-hygiene theory:	http://mnd.tools/51-1
Find out more about Maslow's hierarchy:	http://mnd.tools/51-2
Learn more about theory X and theory Y:	http://mnd.tools/51-3
Find out about Sirota's three-factor theory:	http://mnd.tools/51-4
Find more about Dan Pink's autonomy, mastery, and purpose framework:	http://mnd.tools/51-5

52. Work Effectively with People from Different Generations (Understand Different Generational Characteristics)

Another important part of understanding what makes your people tick is to be conscious of their ages and experiences in the workplace and how this affects their views of the world.

Much of the advice in this book is based on the golden rule: We should treat others the same way we want others to treat us. This goes back to antiquity, and it is present in many different cultures and religions. It's a rule that can help us all, in everyday life and at work. (Sometimes we need to give firm feedback and make tough decisions. However, we can do this in a humane way.)

This is a great starting point for understanding other people, but we can go astray if we apply it too rigidly. For example, cultural differences across countries can be a rich source of misunderstanding, and it is important to be sensitive to these (we discuss this in #64). Another area of difference, and the focus here, is between people from different generations. Many writers have argued that there are significant differences between US baby boomers (born between 1946 and 1964), generation X (1965–1979) and generation Y (1980–1995), and these differences have a big impact on the motivations, interests, and expectations around work.

- ◆ In the United States, baby boomers started out in a workplace that was largely white and male. It is now much more diverse – in gender and ethnicity, in areas such as gay marriage and transgender rights, and in cultural heritage. Younger employees from generations X and Y, who were brought up in this new world, tend to have more socially liberal values, as well as higher self-esteem, self-confidence, and creativity.

- ◆ Baby boomers grew up in a stable workplace with reliable career paths, where people were expected to "pay their dues" before moving into more interesting jobs. Gen Yers' experiences have been much less stable, meaning that their bonds with organizations may be weaker. They are often focused on rapid career advancement, and they can be more individualistic and self-focused than older generations, with more willingness to change jobs and follow nonstandard career paths.

- ◆ Technological change, and the Internet in particular, has had a huge impact on how members of the younger generation make sense of the world. Gen Yers are often called "digital natives" because they grew up with consoles and keypads in their hands. Not only does this change the way they interact with others, but it also potentially makes them more capable than they may have been in the past, and perhaps less trusting of authority figures.

- ◆ Another interesting observation from research highlights changing attitudes to feedback and recognition. Baby boomers are less used to it and may not naturally expect to give much of it, whereas Gen Yers are used to huge amounts of (mostly positive) feedback, and they often expect it in real time.

Although these differences are important, a couple of points of caution are needed. First, in addition to these differences, there are things that stay more or less the same across generations. For example, research suggests that people of all generations value a good work–life balance. Everyone wants to be challenged and involved in decision making. Most people enjoy teamwork and collaboration, and who doesn't want to be fairly rewarded for the work they do?

Second, some observers have said that generational differences are overstated – they say we are simply observing differences between younger and older employees in the same workplace rather than generational shifts. They also suggest that by pandering to the supposed needs of the younger Gen Y employees, we run the risk of creating a self-fulfilling prophecy.

But assuming there is some truth to these arguments (and we believe there is), how can you use them to become a better boss? The answer is simply to factor them into your style of managing so that you can adapt to the particular expectations of the people who work for you. For example, if you are a baby boomer and you are managing a group of Gen Y employees, don't assume they see a stable, long-term role as a good thing; instead, see if you can be creative in offering them new opportunities in different areas. Also, don't resist their preference for working virtually or through microblogging sites (Gen Yers think e-mail is very old school), and be more proactive in giving recognition and praise.

If you can do this as a manager, not only will you be a better boss, but you'll also be much better at attracting talented people to your team and keeping hold of them once they're on board. This will make a huge difference to your team's performance!

Find out more about generational differences: http://mnd.tools/52

53. Develop Emotional Intelligence

To be an effective manager, you need to be able to set a good example and know how to motivate and manage people as individuals. However, there's more that you need to do to be a manager people *want* to follow rather than one they *have* to follow; and this is where the idea of emotional intelligence is useful.

Popularized by Daniel Goleman in his 1996 book, emotional intelligence (EQ) is about being aware of and managing your own emotions and then dealing with others in a positive and skillful way.

Managers who are not emotionally intelligent can be painful to work for – they can be volatile and unrealistic, they can fail to pick up on problems, and they create as many problems as they solve. No one wants to work for a manager like this, and such managers struggle to motivate their teams and retain good people. Meanwhile, managers with high EQ earn huge respect and support, and they find it easy to inspire people to achieve great things.

So what is EQ, and how can you develop it? Goleman describes five elements:

1. **Self-awareness** – People with high EQ are attuned to their own emotions and intuition. They "listen" to what their emotions are telling them and respond to the often insightful messages these convey. They are aware of their own strengths and weaknesses, and they manage these intelligently. Note that we looked at self-awareness in Chapter 1 – the big five personality model (which addresses openness, conscientiousness, extroversion, agreeableness, and neuroticism), personal SWOT (strengths, weaknesses, opportunities, and threats) analysis, journaling, and cognitive restructuring are all helpful ways of developing it.

2. **Self-regulation** – This is all about controlling your emotions and avoiding careless, impulsive decisions. We looked at this in Chapter 3 – stress diaries help you keep the stress you experience under control, the STOP method (stop, think, be objective, and plan) is a way of controlling your anger, and the inverted-U model helps you regulate the level of pressure you are under.

3. **Motivation** – People with high EQ are self-motivated – they know what they want, and they act to make it happen. Goal setting and self-confidence (#3 and #4) are the foundations for this, and we discussed the underlying theory of motivation above.

4. **Empathy** – This is the capacity to engage with the wants, needs, and emotions of the people around you. Empathy helps you understand what motivates them and how to address their needs. Clearly, listening effectively (#50) is

a key part of this, as is paying attention to nonverbal communication. See the URLs below for more on this and other ways of developing empathy.

5. **Social skills** – These are about communicating effectively (see Chapter 11), resolving conflict effectively (#76), being appropriately assertive, and showing high levels of personal integrity (again, see the URLs below for more).

Emotional intelligence is a very broad concept, and as we noted above, it includes many of the specific skills and concepts described in this book. Developing these skills takes practice and experience, but they are all important elements of becoming an effective, respected manager.

Find out more about developing emotional intelligence:	http://mnd.tools/53-1
Learn more about developing empathy:	http://mnd.tools/53-2
Find out how to understand nonverbal communication:	http://mnd.tools/53-3
Discover how to be appropriately assertive:	http://mnd.tools/53-4
Learn how to demonstrate personal integrity:	http://mnd.tools/53-5

Source: Adapted from Goleman 1995. Reproduced with permission of Pearson Education, Inc.

54. Motivate People to Go above and beyond (Transformational Leadership)

The techniques discussed in this chapter will take you a long way in terms of understanding and motivating people. But to get the very best from them, you need to go a bit further – you need to engage their passion and sense of meaning in life. This is where the notion of transformational leadership is useful.

Think about it from your own perspective. There are many factors that affect how hard you work, including the nature of the work itself, the extent to which you find it interesting, and the quality of your relationship with your colleagues. But in addition to all these factors, your boss's leadership skills are also likely to factor into the equation: Some bosses, for reasons we may not completely understand, inspire us to go that extra mile while others leave us cold.

According to influential psychologist Bernard Bass, there are four main things that you need to do to become a transformational leader:

1. **Lead by example.** You are a strong role model for the ethics, conduct, and behaviors you want from the people you lead, and this inspires people to identify with you and to want to emulate you (we looked at this in #49).

2. **Stimulate your people intellectually.** You push your people to be the best they can be by discussing ideas openly, challenging their assumptions in nonthreatening ways, pushing them to look at situations differently, and encouraging them to innovate. What's more – you support your people even when things go wrong as long as they work hard and do their honest best. We looked at some of the opportunities for doing this in Chapters 6–10.

3. **Help your people grow as individuals.** Get to know your people as individuals, pay attention to how they want to grow, and mentor and support them to help them reach their full potential. We'll look at this more in Chapters 12 and 13.

4. **Inspire your people with a compelling vision of the future.** By helping your team understand how the organization makes the world a better place, you provide a positive, attractive vision of the future that their hard work will help to realize. The good news is that many businesses – from refuse collection to food distribution to white goods manufacturing – have real meaning to them if you look for it (see #26 and #27 for translating mission statements down to the individual level).

Think about times in the past when you've been led by someone who uses this approach – it's so inspiring, and you probably worked very hard for this person. The great thing is that *you* can be this type of inspirational boss, and you can motivate this type of passion in your people as long as you put in the hard work needed for it.

Learn more about how to become a transformational leader: http://mnd.tools/54

Other Techniques for Understanding and Motivating Other People

Two key skills and techniques – reading body language and perspective taking – didn't make the cut in our survey when it comes to understanding and motivating other people. These are still highly important, and you can find out more about them at http://mnd.tools/c9c.

Chapter 10

Get the Best from Members of Your Team

B uilding on the previous chapter, your primary purpose as a boss is to get the best from your team. If Chapter 9 was focused on what *you* do as a boss to motivate and inspire those around you, this chapter shifts the emphasis to what your team members do. In other words, it is about how you structure their roles and responsibilities and define the appropriate interventions so that they can work to the best of their abilities.

It is often said that managing others is an "unnatural act" – that is, it requires us to behave in ways that don't come easily to us. Many managers are promoted through the organization because they are high performers. They did their previous job well, they delivered results, and they enjoyed the praise and recognition that came with success. But as soon as these people are given significant managerial responsibilities, they are expected to develop a completely different set of skills – for example, delegating interesting projects to others, putting them in the spotlight and praising them for doing a good job, and investing time more generally in the "people" rather than "task" aspects of work.

It should be no surprise that many managers struggle with this transition. Learning how to get work done *through others* takes time, and many managers never master skills such as effective delegation. When you see a dysfunctional workplace, a common root cause of the problems is senior managers who insist on being involved in everything because they haven't understood the basic principles of delegation and accountability. As noted by management thinker Charles Handy, you should never steal someone else's decisions.

This chapter provides some specific advice on how to get the best from your team. We start by describing practical tips for delegating effectively (#55). Then we provide a useful framework (RACI) to help you clarify who is accountable for what (#56).

These techniques focus on specific roles and responsibilities. We also provide three techniques for improving how you relate to others. Giving people effective praise and recognition (#57) for doing a good job is a well-established way of enhancing their self-esteem and encouraging greater effort in the future. Building the self-confidence of team members (#58) is a broader set of techniques for developing the skills and motivations of those around you. Finally, we describe Heron's six categories of intervention (#59), a framework that helps you think about the right ways to support individuals in your team, depending on the specific circumstances they are facing.

55. Delegate Effectively

Delegation is one of the most important skills you need to develop as a manager. There are only so many hours in a day, and there's only so much work that one individual can do. As your career advances, you become responsible for getting more and more done, and beyond a certain level, the only way to do this is to delegate significant chunks of work to other people.

There's another reason why delegating effectively is good practice: namely, that it is good for the people who work for you. Most people crave some level of control over their own work. Or to put it the other way around, constant micromanagement from above, with the boss overseeing your every move, is annoying and demotivating. Delegation, when done well, is the best means of giving people the autonomy they desire. It allows them to use their intellect and their skills to deliver strong results that make the best use of their strengths.

So if delegation is so important, why do people struggle with it? First, it's a skill, and like all other skills, you need to work at it. Second, you, as the person delegating a job, remain accountable for its successful delivery. This means that you need to build up trust that the person you're delegating to will do a good job, and this takes time.

The starting point for delegation is to look at the work that you do and think about what you can delegate. Keep an activity log (#8) for a couple of weeks, and then review it to see which tasks you could delegate. Think about which members of your team you could delegate these to – you should look for someone who can get up to speed on the necessary skills quickly, and who has the time and motivation to do the job well. (If several people have the necessary skills, delegate the work to the person at the lowest level; otherwise, you'll overload your highest performers with mundane jobs.)

Then, discuss with them what you want them to do. Agree and document the following:

1. The outcome you want to see and how this contributes to the team's mission.
2. The authority level they have. Should they follow precise instructions? Should they recommend a course of action and get it approved by you before going ahead? Should they do what they think is right and then report results, or should they just get on with the job?
3. The resources, support, and training available to them.
4. The goals and deadlines they need to work to.
5. When you will meet to review progress.
6. Any boundaries for the task – things they must not do.

Keep in mind that when you first delegate to someone, the work will take longer to complete than you normally expect it to, and it will rarely be done exactly as you intended. (Be canny about this, and quietly build time for any rework needed into any project schedule that you have agreed upon.) But by providing feedback, you will see quicker and better results the second or third time around. With each successful iteration, you will be able to trust the person more and need to monitor him or her less. But remember that you are ultimately accountable for the successful delivery of the task – you can't abdicate responsibility for getting it done well.

Learn more about delegation, including downloading a
delegation worksheet: http://mnd.tools/55

56. Be Clear About Who Is Accountable for What (The RACI Matrix)

The issue of accountability becomes particularly important when you delegate work to a team of people. It's easy for even highly motivated, hardworking people to get muddled over who is accountable for delivering the task. If people are very busy, they often assume that others are taking care of particular details, meaning that no one attends to them and the delivery fails.

This is why you need to be completely clear about who is responsible for what when you delegate a task to multiple people. The RACI matrix is a useful way of defining the different roles people play around a given task or project:

Responsible – These people do the work needed to deliver it. Multiple people can be responsible.

Accountable – An individual owns the task and "the buck stops" with her and her alone. She is responsible for making sure that the task happens, and she signs off on its successful completion.

Consulted – These people need to give input into the task, and the accountable people need to make sure this consultation happens.

Informed – These people need to be kept up to date on progress, but they have no other role in the delivery.

You can use the RACI matrix to break down a task into subtasks and then identify who is responsible and accountable for each of these. Figure 10.1 shows a sample RACI matrix for a marketing campaign.

Here, Lakshmi is the senior stakeholder who commissioned the campaign – he needs to be consulted over the concept and plan, and he needs to know that the project is being delivered with the right level of quality. Michelle is the marketing manager and is accountable for the successful delivery of the campaign. Juan is a sales manager and will be delivering the campaign's webinars, and Elena is a marketing executive supporting it. By mapping the campaign in this way, it is clear who is responsible for what, and it confirms what Michelle and Juan are individually accountable for.

Subtask	Lakshmi	Michelle	Juan	Elena
Project management	C	A,R	C	C
Campaign concept	C	A,R	R	R
Write white paper	C	A,R	C	R
Create/present webinar	I	C	A,R	
Write mailer copy	I	A	C	R

FIGURE 10.1 **Example RACI Matrix for a Marketing Campaign**
Source: Adapted from Project Management Institute 2017 (PMBOK Guide).

Tip

Use of a RACI matrix implies a top-down, detail-oriented management style. This is appropriate in some situations and not appropriate in others. If you have an experienced and highly skilled team, you'll probably want to let team members self-organize to deliver the project. Even then, someone will need to be accountable for the successful delivery of the project.

Learn more about RACI matrices: http://mnd.tools/56

57. Give Effective Praise and Recognition

Another way you can help your people flourish is to give them effective praise and recognition. As managers, we often focus on negatives – identifying problems and fixing things that are going wrong. There is a good, historic explanation for this. Humans evolved in an environment where we needed to focus our attention on every tiny warning indicator around us so that we could survive. As a result, our brains are "wired" to focus on negatives.

But to be effective as managers of others, we need to take *their* needs into account, and often that means doing things that don't come naturally to us. One such example is providing positive reinforcement, praise, and recognition to those who are doing a good job.

All of us love well-deserved praise, even if we sometimes feel a bit embarrassed by it. Praise causes a neurotransmitter called dopamine to be released in our brains – it gives us a warm glow of satisfaction when we achieve a goal and again when we receive recognition from someone else for having achieved it. We want to get that feeling again!

Think back to your own experience of receiving sincere praise, perhaps from a teacher or a manager. How did you feel about that person? And how much harder did you work for him or her? The research firm Gallup has identified significant increases in helpfulness, cooperation, punctuality, attendance, and length of service associated with receiving regular praise.

In contrast, recall a manager who gave little praise. You probably felt unappreciated, you were less than happy, and you may not have performed to the best of your ability (there are exceptions, but research shows that this is true for the majority of people).

So even if you received little praise yourself as a child, make sure that you give plenty of it now. Make it a practice when you walk around to keep an eye out for things going right, and make sure you compliment people sincerely when you see such things. Be specific about what you're praising, and do it in an appropriate way (some people love public praise; others are embarrassed by it and would prefer to hear your compliments in private).

Tips

- ◆ Be alert to differing cultural attitudes around praise. People in the United States are very used to it, and it's important to give plenty of it when working here. People in some other countries – for example, Germany – may perceive someone giving a lot of praise as being insincere.
- ◆ Also, make sure that the praise you give is honest and proportionate. Insincere praise will weaken trust.

Learn more about giving praise: http://mnd.tools/57

58. Build Team Members' Self-Confidence

One of the benefits of honest praise is that it improves a person's self-confidence. This in turn affects how happy they are, how much initiative they show, and whether they stick with a problem until it's resolved. Clearly, this is a key difference between success and failure for many tasks.

We looked at the importance of personal self-confidence in #4, and we saw the difference between self-efficacy, which relates to a specific type of work, and self-esteem, which is a more general sense that we can cope with what's going on in our lives.

You can help your team members develop self-confidence in much the same way you do for yourself. In other words, you can help them understand and capitalize on their strengths, set clear goals for the future (including ones that will build these strengths), reflect on their successes in the past, and build the skills and connections they need to be recognized as the right person for the job. There are other things you can do as well; for example:

1. **Create "mastery experiences" for them.** Set small goals that allow them to demonstrate to you and to themselves that they have mastered a skill. Then set progressively harder challenges to help them develop their skills further.

2. **Give them the training and information they need to succeed.** Teach them the right way to do tasks, and make sure they have the information and equipment to perform them successfully.

3. **Pair them with experienced role models.** As we saw in #49, people learn a huge amount by watching how skilled, successful people deal with problems and issues. Pair new, inexperienced, or underconfident people with good role models so that they can learn from them and get the coaching and guidance they need to become more confident.

4. **Encourage them.** Tell them when they've done a good job, and make sure to express faith in their abilities when they're struggling.

5. **Provide an environment in which they can succeed.** Allow them to develop new skills without distractions; and manage the amount of pressure they face, so that they have

enough to motivate them to do a good job but not so much that they "fall apart" under it. (See the inverted-U model in #17.)

Tip

Just as we need to avoid shallow overconfidence in ourselves, we need to keep our people grounded, and help them develop appropriate levels of self-confidence. Do this by giving plenty of feedback and by using the approaches we've described. Also, make them aware of the Dunning-Kruger effect – the tendency to overestimate our own abilities when our competence is low and overestimate other people's skills when our competence is high. Find out more about this using the link below.

Find out more about building self-confidence in your
people: http://mnd.tools/58-1
Learn about the Dunning-Kruger effect: http://mnd.tools/58-2

59. Support Your People Effectively (Heron's Six Categories of Intervention)

There are many ways you can support your people, from offering encouragement, as we saw above, to providing a shoulder to cry on when things are going badly.

However, there's more that you can do, and this is where it helps to know about John Heron's six categories of intervention. These are:

1. **Prescriptive** – Give advice and direction, say how people should behave, and tell them what to do to solve a problem.
2. **Informative** – This is about helping people understand a situation – for example, by explaining the underlying principles behind a situation or by sharing an experience.
3. **Confronting** – This involves highlighting behaviors and attitudes that people may not have thought about and getting them to consider whether they are appropriate. It's also about

helping people avoid repeating mistakes. We'll look at two tools for doing this in Chapter 12 – the SBI feedback model (#68) and the GROW model (#69).

4. **Cathartic** – Here, you help your team members express thoughts and emotions they may not have confronted in the past, you empathize with them, and you help them think about how they can deal with a situation.

5. **Catalytic** – This involves encouraging people to reflect on the situation and learn for themselves so they can become more self-directed in how they solve problems.

6. **Supportive** – Finally, supportive interventions build people's confidence by focusing on what they do well, giving honest praise, and showing that you trust in their abilities. This is all about encouraging people when they're struggling.

Clearly, the first three types of intervention are quite autocratic (Heron's authoritative interventions). Although the outcome may be positive, the person being helped can feel uncomfortable, and you may feel awkward using these approaches.

The second group of three (Heron's facilitative interventions) are about helping people develop their own solutions and become more autonomous as individuals. These are much gentler and easier to use, but sometimes they just don't do the job.

Don't back away from giving the "tough love" of authoritative interventions when you need to!

Tip

Providing emotional support can be the last thing you want to do, particularly if you're feeling emotionally exhausted yourself or if someone comes across as "being needy." Make sure that you get help from HR advisors in situations like these – they can be very skilled at helping people solve problems the right way.

Learn more about Heron's six categories of intervention: http://mnd.tools/59

Other Ways to Get the Best from Members of Your Team

One important technique that narrowly missed being included in our top 100 was getting the right balance between laissez-faire management and micromanagement. Find out how to do this at http://mnd .tools/c10c.

Chapter 11

Communicate Effectively

I n the previous chapter, we described a set of techniques for under-standing and motivating people and supporting them so they can do their best work. Here, we put the spotlight on a particular set of skills every good boss needs: namely, well-developed communication skills. Although there are many styles that work – from the flamboy-ant to the understated – there are some common themes that all good communicators share. This chapter focuses mostly on these points of substance to give you some very practical advice on improving your written and oral communication.

The starting point for effective communication is perspective-taking – putting yourself in the shoes of the recipient of your message. For the most part, the people to whom you are communicating are busy and easily distracted. Their scarcest resource is their own atten-tion. If an e-mail is confusing, they will ignore it and move on. If a talk is boring, they will quickly look down at their smartphones. Your job is to hold their attention for long enough to get your message across. It's as simple as that.

We start with the seven Cs – the key principles of good communi-cation (#60). These were developed before the Internet came along, but they are as relevant today as they ever were. We discuss them here particularly in the context of written communication, but they could apply equally to oral communication.

We then discuss two practical techniques. One is learning how to speak well in public (#61) by preparing carefully and working on your delivery. The other is writing effective e-mails (#62), a skill that many people still struggle to master, even though we typically send dozens of e-mails every day.

We finish the chapter with two broader techniques for communicating in an interactive way, rather than through the mostly one-way medium of a speech or e-mail. One is building "high-quality connections" with people at all levels (#63) to help you get closer to them and to build trust. The other is communicating effectively across cultures (#64), which we discuss using the classic framework of Dutch sociologist Geert Hofstede.

60. Understand the Key Principles of Good Communication (The Seven Cs of Communication)

When we communicate, it is smart to be humble in our approach and focus on the needs of our audience. That way, we're much more likely to achieve our goal, which is to get our message across.

Unfortunately, it's all too easy to indulge our own egos by writing in a complex, dense way that seeks to impress people with our knowledge and expertise. We may appeal to a tiny audience of experts and enthusiasts if we do this, but we will lose our wider audience.

This is when it's useful to have the seven Cs of communication – used for many years in the public relations industry – in mind when you're crafting your message. According to the seven Cs, a written message should be:

1. **Complete** – Your message should contain all the information your recipients need and answer common questions they might have. When talking about something that has happened, you need to convey the who, what, when, where, and why. If you want them to do something, you need a clear call to action.

2. **Clear** – Use words carefully and precisely. Use short rather than long words. Break complex sentences down into simple ones.

3. **Concise** – You should keep your message as short as possible, with no unnecessary words or details. Members of your audience are busy and easily distracted.

4. **Concrete** – Keep your message grounded in reality. Focus on facts, figures, actions, and strong images rather than on ideas and generalities.

5. **Considerate** – Focus on the needs of the recipients. You need to get inside their minds: Understand what they want, and give it to them the way they want it.

6. **Courteous** – You need to understand the value system of members of your audience and craft your message in a way that respects this.

7. **Correct** – Accuracy is important, as are spelling, punctuation, grammar, and flow. Make sure you double-check all these things and that your data come from a reputable source. If your organization has a style guide, use it.

Find out more about the seven Cs, including finding out
about other variants: http://mnd.tools/60

Source: Adapted from Cutlip and Center 1952. Reproduced with permission of Pearson Education, Inc.

61. Speak Well in Public

Whether we're delivering webinars, presenting plans to senior managers, contributing in a meeting, or briefing our teams, we all need to speak in public from time to time. Even the most experienced presenters can feel a burst of adrenaline when they do this, but for some, it's terrifying!

It is right that we feel some nerves when speaking in public. These are "moments of truth" that help us look good when we speak well and reflect badly on us if we stumble or say the wrong things. The good news is that, with preparation and practice, you can learn how to control your nerves and be a highly effective public speaker. Go through these stages when you are delivering a speech:

1. TAKE PLENTY OF TIME TO PREPARE

You need a firm grasp of your subject, and this comes from having researched it properly and having made sure that the information you're going to present is robust and accurate. You also need to plan your speech well: Think about the people who make up your audience and what they already know. Will they be well-disposed to your message? What will they want from it, and how should you best deliver this?

Then focus on the structure of your message. Tools such as the rhetorical triangle and Alan Monroe's motivated sequence (see the URLs below) provide structure and help you to craft a compelling message. Business storytelling can help you make powerful points.

2. POLISH YOUR SPEECH, GET PLENTY OF REHEARSAL, AND PLAN FOR ANY PROBLEMS

Write out your speech, then read it out aloud, and tweak the words or slides until you can present smoothly.

Then, rehearse several times so that it starts to come naturally. Some people prepare cue cards with keywords to jog their memory; others put concise bullet points on slides to provide structure. Keep rehearsing until what you're saying flows easily. It can also help to video yourself to identify and eliminate any gestures or habits that could annoy your audience.

If you're going to take questions, think about what the most likely and most difficult questions might be, and rehearse your responses.

Finally, make sure that nothing will surprise you on the day. Visit the place where you're speaking beforehand. Have a backup plan in case of equipment failure or breakdown. If you're presenting slides, make sure your laptop can interface with projectors and audio equipment. And prepare the space appropriately so that you can give your best performance.

3. MANAGE YOUR ADRENALINE, SPEAK CONFIDENTLY, AND ENJOY THE EXPERIENCE!

In the minutes before the performance, expect to feel adrenaline flowing in your body. Calm yourself by breathing deeply and using appropriate relaxation techniques. You may also find yourself worrying about the speech – this is where it helps to think positively, visualize success, and remind yourself that the speech is "all about them" rather than you. Also, remind yourself of how thoroughly you have prepared – this should really help your confidence.

When it is time to speak, stand up straight, relax your muscles, and look members of your audience in the eyes. Don't worry if you don't feel fluent – people mentally edit what other people say, so you'll sound a lot more eloquent than you might think.

You should generally avoid reading your speech word for word. Speak from memory, and use the cue cards you've prepared. If you've

done your preparation and rehearsed often enough, you'll come out really well, and hopefully you'll enjoy the experience!

Find out more about the rhetorical triangle:	http://mnd.tools/61-1
Learn more about Monroe's motivated sequence:	http://mnd.tools/61-2
Learn how to tell effective business stories:	http://mnd.tools/61-3
Find out more about speaking well in public:	http://mnd.tools/61-4

62. Write Effective E-Mails

Used well, e-mail is a wonderful communication channel that allows us to share information quickly, give precise instructions, and encourage others to take action. Used poorly, it's a waste of time and an annoyance.

Many of us receive several hundred e-mails a day, and sifting through them to find important requests or nuggets of information can impose a huge workload on us. No one enjoys wading through poorly constructed e-mails to achieve "inbox zero."

So, when you send an e-mail, make sure it is easy to read, process, and answer. Here are some useful tips:

1. **Don't over-communicate by e-mail.** Don't send e-mails when you can get a quicker answer by talking to someone. Don't e-mail when your message is complex and could be misunderstood – have a meeting instead. Above all, don't send e-mails that could upset people – you need to communicate messages like this in person so you can observe the other person's reaction and correct the situation if your message gets taken the wrong way.

2. **Have a clear, concise subject line.** Briefly summarize what the e-mail's about, put in a deadline date if there is one, and indicate the level of priority. This helps recipients decide whether to open the e-mail.

3. **Focus on one subject.** For example, don't ask questions about a project and then discuss an HR issue in the same e-mail. Your recipient is likely to address your first subject well and miss the second subject entirely. Instead, send separate e-mails, or at least number your points.

4. **Keep your e-mail brief and to the point.** Give recipients the information they need, but keep the e-mail as short as

possible. People expect to pick up the essence of an e-mail in a few seconds, so long or complex ones often get set aside for later.

5. **Be polite, and check for tone.** Before sending, read the e-mail from the recipient's perspective. Make sure the tone is positive and that nothing could be misunderstood or taken the wrong way. It's horribly easy to upset people with a rushed or poorly considered e-mail.

6. **Proof your e-mail carefully.** Check for spelling, grammar, and punctuation. People at all levels will judge your professionalism and attention to detail by this, so make sure their judgment is positive.

Learn more about writing effective e-mails, including seeing examples of these points: http://mnd.tools/62

63. Build Good Working Relationships with People at All Levels (Create "High-Quality Connections")

To communicate effectively with people, we need to create open, trusting relationships with them so they'll be receptive to our messages, just as we will be to theirs. How can we build these "high-quality connections"?

According to psychologist Jane Dutton, building high-quality connections – including developing strong work friendships – helps us to be more productive at work, healthier and less prone to stress, more engaged, and generally more successful. She says we build high-quality connections by:

1. **Engaging respectfully with people.** This involves being punctual; being mentally present when you're engaging with them; being warm, honest, and authentic when you talk; listening mindfully; and communicating in a positive, adult-to-adult way.

2. **Helping others.** This is about encouraging and supporting others – for example, by sharing knowledge or directly helping them achieve their goals. Perhaps we introduce them to others as they integrate with a new organization and help them network with our contacts in a new industry. Or maybe

we flex our schedule to help them do their job while also dealing with challenges in their home lives.

3. **Building trust.** Trust involves showing integrity and being dependable ourselves while also believing the people we're working with will do the same. We show trust to others when we're inclusive, when we delegate work to them, when we ask for feedback, and when we're (intelligently) open about our shortcomings in front of them.

If you are not already doing these things with the people around you, work on them. Sure, it takes a bit of thought and effort, but the benefits of building great working relationships can be enormous!

Tip

Building trust isn't the same thing as being naïve. When money and serious personal advantage is involved, even the most trustworthy people can become "unreliable" in some circumstances. The key is to handle situations professionally so that risks are managed sensibly and appropriate controls are in place.

It's also worth being aware that some people genuinely are out only for themselves. Be aware of the "dark triad" traits of narcissism, Machiavellianism, and psychopathy – you can find out more about these below.

Find out more about building high-quality connections: http://mnd.tools/63-1

Learn more about the dark triad at work: http://mnd.tools/63-2

Source: Adapted from Dutton 2003. Reproduced with permission of John Wiley & Sons, Inc.

64. Communicate Effectively Across Cultures (Hofstede's Cultural Dimensions)

Cross-cultural communication is one of the subtler skills that managers have to wrestle with, and this has become particularly important in recent years with the emergence of a much more diverse workforce, virtual teamwork, and global supply chains.

We're all aware that there are differences between people of different countries and cultures, and we've seen how much conflict can be caused by these differences. So it pays to develop cross-cultural sensitivity and to understand how your own culture differs from others'.

Geert Hofstede's cultural dimensions model provides a useful way into cross-cultural management. Developed over several iterations since the 1970s, the latest version of the model compares national cultures across six dimensions:

1. **Power distance** – This refers to the degree of inequality between people with and without power. People in high power distance countries, such as Malaysia or India, tend to be deferential to authority and are unlikely to initiate action without permission from the boss. In contrast, people in low power distance countries, such as the United Kingdom or New Zealand, are more likely to show initiative, welcome delegation, and want to be involved in decision making.

2. **Individualism/collectivism** – This describes the extent to which people in a society are integrated into groups. Countries such as the United States are relatively individualistic, so people are expected to be self-reliant, they are used to taking personal initiative, and they are comfortable doing business with people they don't know. In contrast, most countries in Asia and South America are relatively collectivist, so they identify strongly with community or work groups, they are happy to conform to group pressure, and they prefer to do business with people they know.

3. **Masculinity/femininity** – This looks at the distribution of roles between men and women, and it highlights the attitude toward traditional gender roles. Japan scores very high in masculinity, so people put a strong emphasis on competition and success, and there are few women in senior executive positions. In contrast, Scandinavian countries such as Sweden score higher on the femininity side of the spectrum, so people tend to work more through consensus, and they put a lot of emphasis on work–life balance.

4. **Uncertainty avoidance** – This refers to how well people cope with anxiety and uncertainty, and how much predictability people want in their lives. Greece and Japan, for example, score very highly on uncertainty avoidance, so people in those countries tend to resist radical change and they are attracted to job security. Singapore and Sweden, in contrast, rate very low on this scale, and people there tend to adapt more readily to major changes in their external environments.

5. **Long-term/short-term orientation** – This refers to how people link the past to the future. It is particularly useful in understanding why some countries develop more quickly than others. For example, China has a long-term orientation that favors thrift and perseverance and adaptation to changing circumstances, whereas African countries such as Ghana and Nigeria have a short-term orientation, where traditions are sacrosanct and behavior is rooted in the past.

6. **Indulgence/restraint** – This is the extent to which people feel free to be themselves and have fun. People in low-indulgence countries, such as Russia, are constrained by social norms and may be pessimistic. By contrast, people in high-indulgence countries, such as the Netherlands, are more likely to value their leisure time, be positive, and have fun.

So how can you use this framework? The first step is to be aware of these differences, which helps you to be more understanding and tolerant of the way people from other cultures behave when you meet them. Many Americans, for example, see people from Asia as passive and shy when they first meet them, but that is likely a reflection of their own individualistic worldview.

A second step: If you want to be more analytical about this, go to the Hofstede website and explore how your own culture compares with the cultures of the people on your team. You need to become a "detective" in such circumstances to figure out which dimensions of culture are most relevant. Remember that Hofstede's analysis is necessarily very general – there are many individuals who do not conform to their national stereotypes.

Finally, on the basis of this improved understanding, you need to be prepared to alter your style of management. For example, some techniques, such as delegation and brainstorming, don't work as well in high power distance or collectivist groups. One of the hallmarks of good bosses is their ability to adapt and to tailor their way of working to the needs of their team.

Find out more about Hofstede's cultural dimensions:	http://mnd.tools/64-1
Compare cultures using Hofstede's website:	http://mnd.tools/64-2

Source: Adapted from Hofstede 2010. Reproduced with permission of Geert Hofstede B.V. http://geerthofstede.com.

Other Techniques for Communicating Effectively

Communication is a huge topic. There are very many skills that you can learn to become a highly skilled communicator, and these include two particularly important ones that didn't make the cut in our survey. Learn more about these at http://mnd.tools/c11c.

Chapter 12

Hire and Develop Good People

A lot of the work you do as a manager is in the here and now – making decisions, solving problems, chairing meetings, and dealing with difficult situations. But as you take a more long-term perspective on your role, it quickly becomes clear that one of your most important jobs is hiring and developing good people. Indeed, one of the best ways to make a lasting impact on your organization is to recruit and surround yourself with highly talented people, so that they in turn attract other good people.

To get people development right, you need to adopt a subtle but important shift in perspective. The traditional logic of management and organization starts with a definition of the work to be done – the work is broken down into specific jobs, and people are then assigned to those jobs. This mechanistic approach is often efficient, but it treats people as replaceable parts, so it rarely gives them the opportunity to achieve their full potential.

The alternative logic is to think of management as "helping your people do their best work." This means focusing first on the skills, motivations, and aspirations of the people working for you and then on how you can harness these to the greatest effect. Of course, you still have to make sure that all the necessary work gets done, but this shift in perspective helps you keep the needs of your people foremost in your mind as you manage them.

In this chapter, we focus on five tools and techniques to help you hire and develop good people. Designing jobs effectively (#65) involves thinking about how a given role links to the broader

142

purpose of the organization and, from this, how it can be structured so that it's intrinsically motivating to the person doing it. Recruiting effectively (#66), likewise, isn't just about finding someone who can tick the boxes in terms of prior experience. Rather, it is about trying to understand the competencies and outlooks candidates have developed. That way, you can bring people into your team with the values and capabilities they need to excel in their new roles and thrive and develop as individuals.

To build a team with the right overall capabilities, a skills matrix can be very useful (#67). This technique allows you to map the capabilities of individuals against the specific skill areas needed to do a good job, so that you can identify development opportunities for specific people and also spot any gaps that need filling.

Giving effective feedback is also a vital part of your role (#68), though most managers say this is not a part of the job they do well, nor is it one they particularly enjoy. We describe the situation–behavior–impact tool as one practical and useful way of providing feedback to individuals. Finally, coaching people (#69) so that they understand and act on opportunities for personal development is a way of helping them to take a longer-term perspective on their work. We describe the GROW model as a useful technique in this area.

In addition to all these specific techniques, you need to remind yourself that your job is to get the best from the people working for you. It is all too easy to lapse into "task mode" and simply allocate people to whatever is easiest or most convenient in the here and now. You need to resist this temptation where possible and look for creative ways of nurturing and developing your people so that they can be the best they can be.

65. Design Jobs Effectively (Motivation-Centered Job Descriptions)

To make a successful hire, you need to start with a clear idea of what you want the person doing the job to do, hence the notion of job descriptions. However, good job descriptions are more than just a list of duties and responsibilities – they anchor the job in the organization's mission, and they provide a sense of why the role is important.

This notion that work should be meaningful has cropped up several times already – in the MPS (meaning, pleasure, and strengths) process (#21), the discussion of transformational leadership (#54), the use of OGSM (objectives, goals, strategies, and measures, #26) and OKRs (objectives and key results, #27) in structuring work, and Herzberg's motivation-hygiene theory (#51.).

To hire good people, it is important to start with a well-developed, motivation-focused job description. To draw up such a job description, follow these steps:

1. **Understand the job in detail.** Clarify the purpose of the job from the perspective of the organization, and talk with existing jobholders to understand the detail of the work they're doing. Analyze the day-to-day activities people perform, the skills and experience they need to do a good job, and the personality profile of those who flourish in the role (#1).

2. **Define the essential results that the person needs to achieve.** Jobs evolve over time, and there can be a gradual divergence between what the individual is doing and what is actually needed. Also, there may be several ways of doing the same thing so that people can achieve the same result in different ways. This is why it helps to focus on defining objectives and key results (#27) rather than specifying precisely how people should do the job.

3. **Write the job description.** Organize your job description into these sections:

    Position identifiers – Clearly identify the job title, the team and department, the job's reporting lines, the job roles reporting to the job holder, and the salary band for the role. Make the job title customer-focused – for example, customer success manager instead of account manager.

    Job purpose – Specify how the role contributes toward the mission of the team and the organization, and condense objectives and key results into an easily understood, inspiring statement of purpose.

    Description of key results – Specify the key results the person should achieve so that he or she has clear goals to work toward and can feel the satisfaction that comes from achieving these goals. As you're doing this, make sure the results you're asking for fit with the personality types of high achievers in the role and that people with these personality types are likely to find that the job attractive.

Competency requirements and competency development – Identify the knowledge, skills, aptitude, education, certifications, and experience levels needed to achieve the key results. And go beyond this to map out the career paths the position can lead to and the skill development you expect jobholders to engage with.

Personal characteristics – Describe the personality traits and values that you're looking for from your new hire and the interpersonal skills they'll need, as well as the skills, education, and experience that are required.

Other requirements – Finally, detail any strenuous or difficult aspects of the work – for example, uncomfortable working conditions, unusual physical demands, nonstandard hours, or extensive travel. These things need to be clear right from the start so that they don't come as an unpleasant surprise when the new person starts work.

With a clear, well thought-out, motivationally focused job description – that is, with a well-designed job – it's much easier to create compelling job advertisements, attract exceptional candidates to your organization, run an effective recruitment process, and get the best from new hires once they're working for you.

Tip

It's essential to work with your HR team when it comes to developing job descriptions – this is a core part of the work they do. For new types of roles, they can draw on standardized job descriptions that give you a good starting point for designing jobs, and they'll ensure that job descriptions comply with national employment legislation. Make sure, though, that motivating factors and the meaning of the role come through clearly in the final copy – it's easy for these to get "watered down" or lost while developing job descriptions, but they *really* matter.

Learn more about designing jobs and writing job
descriptions: http://mnd.tools/65

---

66. Recruit Effectively (Competency–Based Interviewing)

Another advantage of developing good, motivation-centered job descriptions is that they help you craft the insightful interview questions you need to select the best candidate for the role.

Competency-based interviewing is an approach to recruiting that emphasizes the actual competencies people need to do a great job. This moves interviews from being loose, unstructured discussions where you just try to "get a feel for the candidate" and turns them into focused exercises where you explore people's competencies, experience, behaviors, and values in detail. Not only does this help you select great candidates for the role, but it also helps you guard against unconscious bias and discrimination.

To plan a competency-based interview, start with the competency requirements section of the job description (#65) you've written. This will list the competencies needed to achieve the key results you've identified. Bear in mind that if you're in a specialized business, few candidates will have all of the competencies you're looking for – what you need to find are people who can easily develop them.

Then, focus on the most important of these competencies for the interview. Many people can "talk the talk" in an interview without being suited for the job at all (this is particularly the case with professional communicators such as managers, salespeople, and marketers). As an interviewer, you need to cut through this by exploring how your interviewees actually behaved in past situations that are like the ones they'll encounter on the job. You need to probe the skills, attitudes, and values they bring to the role so that you can understand how they are likely to behave in similar situations, particularly when they are under pressure.

This is where it's useful to structure your questions using the SOAR acronym – situation, objective, actions, and results. For example, if you want to explore how well people set and achieve personal goals (competency), your question might be: Give me an example of something significant that you are proud of achieving (situation). What did you set out to do and why (objective)? What did you do to achieve it, what obstacles did you overcome, and how did you overcome them (actions)? And what happened in the end (result)?

By asking questions in a structured, open-ended way like this, you encourage interviewees to talk – and reveal a great deal about their values, their abilities, and their strengths and weaknesses. You can also ask supplementary questions – for example, "Why did you do that?" or "How did people react?" This brings out even more information on how the person is likely to behave in your workplace.

Tip

Competency-based interviewing gives you great insights, but you shouldn't rely on it completely. You should also walk through people's résumés to understand their qualifications, their experience, and the story of their careers, particularly with reference to why they moved from job to job.

It's also fundamentally important to test skill levels and evaluate the quality of their work. This helps you separate the many people who are confident but lacking competence from those who can do a good job for you.

Learn more about competency-based interviewing, including other types of questions: http://mnd.tools/66-1

Explore different interview questions you can use when hiring people: http://mnd.tools/66-2

Find out more about using "inbox testing" to test people's skills: http://mnd.tools/66-3

67. Assess Individual Development Needs (Skills Matrices)

Once you've assembled a good team, the next stage is to provide them with the opportunities to develop so that they have the skills to perform effectively. After all, few people arrive "fully formed" for a job.

It is useful to create a skills matrix to think about skill levels across your team, and this gives you a great starting point for planning how you'll develop your people. You can see an example of a skills matrix in Figure 12.1.

This is a simple table with the skills people need for success shown as column headings and their names shown as rows down the left-hand side. In each cell, you put an assessment of how skilled the person is at that type of task. (In this example, 0 means an individual doesn't have a particular skill, 1 means they have the skill at a basic

0	No skills	1	Learned	2	Expert

Team: Administration		**Manager:** Reginald			**Date:** March 23, 20XX		
		Research Skills			**Presentation Skills**		
Team	**Job**	Census	BMD	Wills & Probate	Writing	Page Layout	Image Rework	**Individual Score**
Jez	Coordinator	2	2	2	2	2	2	**12/12**
Alun	Agent	2	2	1	1	2	1	**9/12**
Tess	Agent	2	1	1	1	1	0	**6/12**
Patti	Agent	1	1	1	2	2	0	**7/12**
Zhen	Assistant	1	1	1	0	0	0	**3/12**
Sally	Trainee	0	0	0	0	0	0	**0/12**
Task Score		**8/12**	**7/12**	**6/12**	**6/12**	**7/12**	**3/12**	
# People Required to Have This Skill		6	6	6	6	3	1	

FIGURE 12.1   **Example Skills Matrix**

level but need practice to develop it further, and 2 means they have developed the skill fully.)

To create a skills matrix for your team, follow these steps:

1. **Identify the skills your people need.** Do this by analyzing job descriptions and by asking the highest performers which skills matter most for them to do their jobs well. Consolidate your list, and write skills as column headings on your table.

2. **List your people and their job titles.** These go down the left-hand side of the table.

3. **Decide how you'll code your table.** Our example has 0 (darkest gray) for no skills, 1 (light gray) for some skills, and 2 (white) for well-developed skills. Another option is to use a red–amber–green coding.

4. **Measure performance levels.** Assess each person's level for each skill. Talk to them about the training and self-development they've done, review their appraisals to understand performance, and observe the quality of their work.

5. **Analyze your matrix and take action.** Look at your matrix, and review whether you have the right people in the right roles and whether a reshuffle might be appropriate. Then, look at the skills each individual needs compared with their current skills, and develop a plan for how you'll develop each person to be fully effective.

6. **Review your matrix regularly.** Keep your good work "alive" by reviewing your matrix regularly and keeping people's development at the forefront of your mind.

Find out more about developing a skills matrix: http://mnd.tools/67

---

68. Give Effective Feedback (The SBI Feedback Model)

A skills matrix helps you think about personal development in a formalized way. This should be complemented with the day-to-day feedback and coaching that you give to individuals in your role as their manager. (We'll look at coaching next in #69.)

Feedback is vital for individual development – it's how people know whether what they're doing is working. This reinforces useful behaviors and gives people the insight they need to change unhelpful ones. This is often all they require to get back on the right track.

However, as a manager, it is very easy to give feedback badly; if you do, it can backfire on you and damage the relationship. It pays to do the following when you give feedback:

Try to give more positive feedback than negative feedback. Whenever you see someone doing something good, tell them. Again, you'll reinforce good behavior, and people will understand that you're on their side when you have to give uncomfortable messages.

Be timely. That way, people can make changes right away, and you can "nip issues in the bud"– before they become serious.

Give feedback often. If you do this, people will get used to it as part of their routines (and it is vastly preferable to the dreaded annual review).

Be specific, and don't generalize. Stick to hard facts. Otherwise, you end up trying to justify your subjective views, which the other person may well challenge, leaving them feeling aggrieved or angry.

Give negative feedback in private. Otherwise, you'll humiliate the person in front of their peers, which has all sorts of negative consequences.

When it comes to giving feedback, there are several different approaches that you can use, which suit different situations. A useful approach is to use the situation–behavior–impact (SBI) tool. Developed by the Center for Creative Leadership, this helps you give powerful, highly specific feedback that is hard to argue with.

1. **Situation** – This defines the context of the feedback and gives people time to recall their memories of the situation. For example, you could say, "This morning, when you came in to work ... " or "In Tuesday's presentation to the leadership team ... "

2. **Behavior** – Describe what you saw accurately, don't rely on hearsay, and don't attribute motives or make judgments. For example, "You came in 15 minutes late" or "Your slides were exceptionally clear and well laid out."

3. **Impact** – Explain the consequences of the action. For example, "This caused you to miss the morning rush, meaning that other members of the team were under so much pressure that they couldn't give our customers the level of service they deserved" or "This made a great impression and helped us to deliver a highly credible presentation."

Tip

If you use SBI, you're likely to get your message across clearly. However, when used to give negative feedback, it can be quite hard-hitting, and it might leave the individual feeling quite upset.

You may want to soften feedback by delivering it as a "sandwich" by layering negative feedback between positive comments. However, this approach can breed cynicism, and some people may just focus on the last thing you've said, leaving your feedback session thinking that everything is okay.

| Learn more about giving feedback effectively: | http://mnd.tools/68-1 |
| Find out more about SBI: | http://mnd.tools/68-2 |

69. Coach People Effectively (The GROW Model)

In some situations, you'll get the behavior change you want just by giving people feedback, and that's great. At other times, you'll need a more formal approach to get change that lasts. This is where the GROW model can help you.

Developed by business coaches Graham Alexander, Alan Fine, and Sir John Whitmore, GROW stands for goal, reality, options, and will, and it's particularly useful for motivating people to change. One key feature is that it encourages people being coached to come up with most of the answers themselves while being guided in the right direction by you, their manager. This helps them take ownership of the plan you arrive at, making it much more likely that they'll do the work needed to deliver change.

1. **Goal** – Start by discussing the behavior that you want to change with your team member (SBI and similar approaches can help here – see #68), and get them to structure this change as a goal. Make sure that this goal is aligned with both the team's objectives and your team member's career development aspirations.

2. **Reality** – Ask them to describe the current reality and its consequences and fully explore the things that may be contributing to this situation, including any goal conflicts the person may be experiencing. As you do this, provide any information he or she may be missing so that you come to a common agreement on what reality is.

3. **Options** – Help your team member brainstorm options for achieving the goal. Encourage them to think widely, identify and consider how to overcome any obstacles along the way, and choose the best options to pursue. This gives them a plan that they can pursue.

4. **Will** – Ask your team member to commit to this plan. Agree on milestone dates by which specific actions need to be completed, and agree on follow-up dates to review progress.

Tip

Conventional coaching theory says you should guide the process, but allow people to come to their own conclusions at each stage. This reflects the fact that many coaches don't know the details of their clients' lives.

As a manager, it's your job to get people to show the right behaviors, and you often have a sharp insight into what's going on. This is where you need to make sure that they draw the correct conclusions, set effective goals, and take the right actions.

Learn more about the GROW model, including exploring
questions you can ask and seeing an example: http://mnd.tools/69-1

Find out more about other coaching techniques: http://mnd.tools/69-2

Chapter 13

Build a Great Team

I n large companies today, a lot of work is done in teams. There are many types of teams – some have a clearly defined leader; others are deliberately nonhierarchical – but the key defining feature is some sort of collective responsibility for outcomes.

In theory, a team should be able to achieve more than a random group of individuals because team members have complementary knowledge and skills. But in reality, teams often end up making poor decisions. Studies of famous political misjudgments (for example, the Bay of Pigs fiasco) and business blunders (such as Time Warner buying America Online) have shown how easy it is for teams to make suboptimal decisions – for example, veering into groupthink or not giving enough voice to minority opinions.

Today, there is lots of research evidence for how to make teams effective. For example, a study at MIT highlighted such things as diversity of team members, equal contribution to discussion, and social skills. And a recent study at Google emphasized the importance of a supportive team environment for producing high-quality outcomes (also called psychological safety).

But even though we know how to build a great team in theory, the challenge of doing it in practice is still considerable. You need to develop real skill as a manager to get the best from your team, and the purpose of this chapter is to suggest some practical ways of building that skill.

The first challenge is to formally define the team's charter (#70) so that it is clear and meaningful to everyone. Ideally, this is done at the point when the team is formed, but it is also useful to review team charters periodically. Once they are up and running, you also need to brief your team clearly (#71), which means communicating effectively about what is happening in the rest of the organization and keeping the team updated on any problems. A related technique is building trust in your team (#72) so that people feel safe to share problems and try out new ideas – without fear of being criticized. And at the heart of everything, there is a need for you to work on your personal relationships with team members so that they understand and trust you. We offer the Johari window as one technique for building openness and self-knowledge (#73).

We then provide some ideas for how to understand team-specific motivation (#74) so that you can be more effective at structuring the work they do to make it as satisfying and engaging as possible. Finally, we look at where teamwork can go wrong by exploring Patrick Lencioni's Five Dysfunctions of a Team.

70. Formally Define the Team's Mission, Authority, Resources, and Boundaries (Team Charters)

When people work well together as a team, they can achieve great things, and the experience can be wonderful for all involved. However, there are also situations where the results are terrible: Passionate people pull in different directions, they argue with one another, they fall out, and they fail to achieve the team's mission, sometimes in a spectacular way.

Sometimes the problems are caused by personality differences. Often, though, it is misunderstandings about the team's purpose and the roles of individuals in achieving it, which is why it's so important to make these things clear right from the start.

You can set your team members up for success by working with them to agree on a team charter. The charter ensures that everyone knows what the team's purpose is, what people's jobs are within it, what the team has the power to do and what it doesn't, and what resources it can draw on. The charter also helps team members agree with one another on how they will work together so that things run smoothly for everyone.

The exact content of your team charter will vary from situation to situation, but it will be most useful when it's negotiated and agreed upon by the people setting the team up, the team leader, and team members. The following headers are often useful:

Context – This explains why the team exists, what problem it needs to solve, and how its work fits with the broader objectives of the organization. (If you're using an OGSM [objectives, goals, strategies, and measures] or OKRs [objectives and key results] – see Chapter 5 – include relevant parts of these here.)

Mission and objectives – This is a short, clear statement of what the team needs to achieve and deliver. It provides focus and helps people decide quickly whether specific activities are contributing to the team's goals.

Stakeholders – This identifies the external stakeholders that the team needs to communicate with and satisfy to achieve its mission.

Composition and roles – This defines the "design" of the team – who will participate in it, what their roles will be, and how much of their time will be allocated to it. In structuring the team, the leader needs to understand people's strengths, weaknesses, skills, and experiences and make sure that the right things are being done by the right people. This is quite a subtle piece of work, and it involves thinking about resourcing levels and team and subteam structure. It also involves making sure that there is appropriately diverse input into problem solving and decision making (see Chapters 6–8 for why this matters) and that all stakeholders are appropriately represented.

Authority and empowerment – This says what the team is able to do under its own initiative and what it must seek permission to do. For example, is it empowered to hire new people? What payment sign-off levels does it have? And can it insist that team members focus on the team's work exclusively? The team's boundaries are also defined here so that the team's work does not conflict with work done by other teams in the organization.

Resources and support available – This defines the resources available to the team (including money, time, equipment, and people) so that team members are aware of and know to use them. This section also defines the training and coaching that are available, as well as external help that the team can draw on.

Operations – This final part of the charter defines how the team will work on a day-to-day basis. This covers such things as when the team meets and what team members will do, the standards of behavior people expect from one another, how decisions will be made, and how they will give feedback to one another.

Some parts of the charter are created by the people setting the team up. The team leader drafts some other parts, and others are written by the team members working together. What's important is that everyone involved has a fair opportunity to challenge and negotiate the draft charter so that there is buy-in to it.

Tip

The best time to create a team charter is when the team is formed. That way, it is set up for success right from the start. However, it can be helpful to create or review a charter if a team is experiencing problems, such as internal conflict. By doing this, you can bring any hidden issues and misunderstandings out into the open and clearly and consensually set behavior standards that everyone can commit to.

Learn more about team charters, including seeing an
example being developed: http://mnd.tools/70

71. Brief Your Team Clearly

A good team charter gives team members the information they need to succeed, right from the start. But teams can't work in isolation:

They need to know what's going on in the organization and the wider world around them so that they can adapt to these changing circumstances.

The best way to provide this context is through regular team briefings. These are short sessions where you update team members on what's happening in the organization, and you then take their questions. These briefings build organizational awareness, they reduce the risk of misunderstandings and gossip, and they help to build trust within the team. To do this effectively:

◆ Run regular briefings, ideally straight after decision-making meetings, so that people get information promptly and directly from you (rather than through the office grapevine).

◆ Keep the briefing focused on the key information people need to know. You can often structure this using the four Ps headings:

> *Progress* – How the team and organization have performed against the target and what progress has been made since the last briefing.

> *Procedures* – Changes to policies or ways of doing things that people need to know about.

> *People* – Who is joining the team or organization? Who is leaving? And are there any people-related changes that people should know about?

> *Points for action* – Priorities that people need to address in the period ahead and actions they need to take.

◆ Take questions, and answer them as openly as you can while still respecting confidentiality. (If there are things you can't discuss, acknowledge this and make it clear that you'll update people when you are able.)

◆ Make sure your team members brief their own teams immediately afterward, and that information ripples down through the organization, so that everyone knows what's going on.

◆ If people have questions you can't answer or have concerns or worries that you can't deal with, follow up on these with your manager, and do what you can to address them after the briefing.

As you're doing this, focus on getting the key messages across to your people, keep your message positive but truthful, and "own the message" – don't try to distance yourself from it.

Find out more about briefing your team effectively: http://mnd.tools/71

---

72. Build Trust in Your Team

By keeping people up to date and being open with them about challenges, you'll start to build trust between yourself and your team.

In simple terms, trust is a belief that others won't exploit your vulnerabilities. In a low-trust environment, people don't take risks and they don't share their problems because they are worried about being criticized or exploited. There will be things that people simply won't do because it leaves them feeling unacceptably exposed. As a result, change fails, productivity declines, innovation falters, and talented people fail to reach their potential – and they leave.

A high-trust environment, in contrast, is one with a lot of give and take, one where you can work efficiently and effectively together. People can be flexible and take intelligent risks while being confident that others around them will support them and look after them. So, how can you achieve this type of high-trust environment in your team?

As with everything, begin with yourself and the way you behave. Work hard to build the skills you need to be effective, develop your emotional intelligence so that you deal with people maturely (#53), and take care with your problem solving and decision making (see Chapters 6 and 7). All of this helps you build your reputation for competence and good judgment so that people trust you to make the right decisions.

At the same time, earn trust by being a model of the integrity you want to see in your people. Keep your promises. Communicate openly and honestly. Support your team members, look out for their interests, and involve them in significant decisions whenever you sensibly can.

It is also smart to avoid placing blame. Mistakes happen, and as long as people have done their best, the right thing to do is to work together to fix the problem and move forward while learning from the situation and making sure it doesn't happen again. (Clearly, where people haven't made their best effort or have acted in a way that isn't aligned with the team's interests, you need to deal with this appropriately.)

Next, get to know your people personally. Take some time to find out about their families and personal interests, and share personal information about your own. Encourage social and team-building events where people can get to know one another as individuals.

Break down cliques within your team by varying work patterns so that different people work with one another, and discuss how harmful it is to have in-groups and out-groups and to have people feeling isolated and unsupported by the rest of the team.

Finally, make sure that people show good team behavior when they deal with one another, that they support other team members, and that they're open, generous, and conscientious in the way they work.

| Learn more about building trust in your team: | http://mnd.tools/72 |

73. Build Openness and Self-Knowledge within a Team (The Johari Window)

Openness is important for building trust, partly because it allows people to get to the root of problems quickly and partly because it helps to make sure that people get plenty of feedback. So how can you build openness in your team? This is where the Johari window, used sensitively, can help people to be more open with one another.

Developed by Joseph Luft and Harry Ingham, the word *Johari* comes from a combination of their names. You can see the Johari window in Figure 13.1.

The Johari window is a way of thinking systematically about how you are known and understood by others. One axis depicts how much you know about yourself; the other depicts how much others know about you. The window is split into four quadrants:

1. **The open area** represents things that you and other people know about you. This includes the way that you behave and

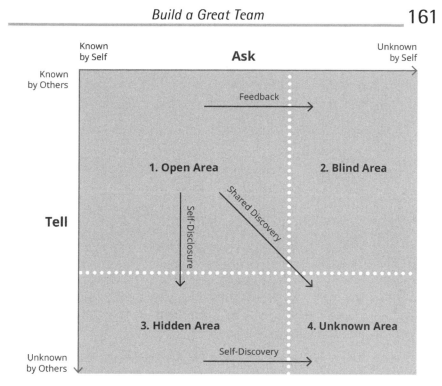

Figure **13.1**   **The Johari Window**
Source: Adapted from Luft 1992.

the knowledge, skills, and personal history that the people
you work with are aware of.

2. **The blind area** contains things that you don't know about
   yourself but others can see. This is where their feedback can
   help you improve the way you work, and it's where you can
   discover talents that you didn't know you had.
3. **The hidden area** represents things that you know about
   yourself but others don't know. You can build trust by disclosing some of these things (but be wise in the way you do
   this).
4. **The unknown area** contains things about you that neither
   you nor others know.

There are two ways of using the Johari window. One is simply
to encourage people to expand the open area of the window by
disclosing harmless information to one another and by asking for and
giving one another feedback. This helps people build understanding

of one another, and it helps them learn about their own strengths. (Do this sensitively: Don't pressure people to make self-disclosures they'll regret, and make sure that feedback is gentle and positive.)

A more systematic approach is to use a list of 56 neutral or positive adjectives that describe people. Each person picks, say, five adjectives that they think best apply to themselves and then they pick five adjectives that apply to each of their peers. These are then inserted into the grid for each person, and people discuss what they can see. This gives plenty of opportunities for self-disclosure and positive, kind feedback, all of which helps to build trust.

Tip

There are times when you need to disclose difficult things and give hard feedback. Do this in private, not as part of a Johari window team-building session.

Find out more about using the Johari window, including a
link to the 56 adjectives: http://mnd.tools/73

74. Find the Specific Motivators That Work Best with Your Team (Understand Team-Specific Motivation)

In Chapter 9 (#51 and #54), we looked at specific techniques and approaches you can use to motivate individuals. It takes a lot of time to use these tools well, but you can make a great start by addressing motivation at a team level. If you can get a handle on the common motivators for people on your team, you can structure the way they interact with each other, which in turn will help them get the best out of their work. Here are the steps to follow:

1. Bring your people together, and get them to write down the things that motivate them as individuals. These could be things such as money, purpose, promotion prospects, recognition, achievement, personal growth, and camaraderie, but they could also include having a nice working environment or flexible working arrangements. Encourage them to come up with as many as possible.

2. Go around the room, with each person listing their most important motivators. Write these on a whiteboard, and consolidate suggestions so that similar things come under the same heading. Then go through each heading, discussing what each one means, so that people come to a common understanding.

3. Next, ask the team to look at the list and write down their top five (say) motivators in order. The top motivator gets five points, the second gets four, and so on down the list.

4. Individuals then write their personal scores against each of these motivators on the whiteboard. By adding these scores up, you can identify your team's top motivators. But you can also see whether there are big differences across the members of the team.

5. Finally, brainstorm how to structure the team's work to deliver on these motivators while also achieving the overall goals. Then, if they make sense, do these things.

By following this approach, you'll see increased team motivation; you'll also find that people take real ownership of the team's working process and commit more strongly to the team.

Tip

What motivates people in a sales team, for example, is likely to differ from what motivates people in finance, engineering, or people/HR teams. If everyone on your team does similar jobs, this adding-up approach is likely to work well. If team members come from different functions, you may want to add up scores separately, by function.

Find out more about team-specific motivation, including
things you can do to address common motivators: http://mnd.tools/74

75. Manage Negative Behaviors and Resolve Conflict (Lencioni's Five Dysfunctions of a Team)

So far in this chapter, we've looked at ways to set your team up for success. However, you also need to keep an eye out for things going wrong, and this is where it helps to be aware of Patrick Lencioni's five dysfunctions of a team. Published in 2002, Lencioni's book suggests five major sources of dysfunctionality:

1. **An absence of trust** – We looked at the importance of trust and how you can build it in #72. A lack of trust manifests itself in a number of ways: People avoid social events and teamwork; they don't ask for help from one another; they cover up mistakes and weaknesses; and they generally withdraw from the team and try to avoid working with one another.

    You can start to deal with these problems by behaving in a trustworthy way yourself, but in addition, you need to deal with the behaviors that are undermining trust. So talk with your team to understand what's going on, and look out for behaviors that threaten the cohesion of the team or individuals within it. You'll need to deal with these firmly – positive measures to build trust won't be effective until you've dealt with the underlying issues.

2. **Fear of conflict** – Conflict within a team is often uncomfortable, but it can also be highly productive when it involves people respectfully testing and challenging one another's ideas, with better ideas emerging as a result.

    Signs of a fear of conflict include people holding their opinions back, avoiding awkward truths during meetings, and talking behind other people's backs. To get past these problems, encourage people to engage in healthy debate, and support them when they do – but make sure that debate is focused on ideas and not on individuals. Also, learn and teach conflict resolution techniques – we'll look at a useful one in #76.

3. **Lack of commitment** – Another downside of people not sharing their ideas is that they may feel they haven't been heard. They may think that plans haven't been discussed

properly, or they may know that conflict hasn't been resolved and they may wait to see "which side wins." As a result, they don't commit to plans, they continue talking and not doing, and opportunities are missed.

Deal with this by getting everyone's input on decisions, clarifying uncertainties where you can, discussing plans thoroughly, and using transparent decision-making approaches. (See Chapter 7; you may also want to use voting approaches such as multivoting or the modified Borda count – see the links below for more on these.)

4. **Avoidance of accountability** – A lack of accountability or "ownership" has predictable negative consequences as team members don't hold one another to high standards, and they don't cover for team members who are struggling.

   Address this problem by clarifying responsibilities with a team charter (#70), running retrospectives (#31), setting up a system of team rewards for the achievement of team goals, and by dealing with poor performance (#79) if people don't take appropriate responsibility.

5. **Inattention to results** – This happens where people have lost focus on the team's goals, perhaps because other objectives have more prominence, perhaps because of infighting, or perhaps because they're more focused on advancing their own careers than they are on the team's mission.

   You can spot this when the team routinely fails to deliver good results, when people are focusing on the wrong goals, and when talented, results-oriented people get frustrated and choose to leave the team.

   Deal with this problem by refocusing team members with a team charter, by reminding them of the OGSM (#26), by setting clear OKRs (#27), and by addressing poor performance if this doesn't work.

Find out more about Lencioni's five dysfunctions of a team:	http://mnd.tools/75-1
Learn about multivoting:	http://mnd.tools/75-2
Discover how to rank subjective options using the modified Borda count method:	http://mnd.tools/75-3

Source: Adapted from Lencioni 2005. Reproduced with permission of John Wiley & Sons, Inc.

Chapter 14

Deal with Difficult Management Situations Effectively

An important theme running through this book is the idea that a great boss is someone who helps and supports their people to do their best work. This worldview encourages us to engage in positive, developmental behaviors such as coaching, delegating, and communicating openly.

But this approach to management assumes that employees have both the will and the skill to do their jobs well. Even if this assumption is valid 95% of the time, we still have to figure out how to act the other 5% of the time.

The reality is that there will always be a small number of people who, for whatever reason, are not interested in doing a good job or lack the basic capability to be effective. They show up late, they shirk, they complain, and they make frequent mistakes – and their negative behaviors create problems for those around them.

One of the hallmarks of a really good boss is the ability to handle these situations quickly and effectively. In many ways, this is the toughest part of the manager's job because it involves dealing with unpleasant situations and making difficult decisions. It is always tempting to duck the difficult choices and to give an individual the benefit of the doubt. But keep in mind that one bad apple spoils the entire bunch – in other words, if you allow one individual to get away with behaving badly, the whole organization suffers. The title of Bob Sutton's best-selling book *The No Asshole Rule* captured this point perfectly.

In this chapter, we discuss five techniques for managing difficult situations. First, we look at interpersonal dynamics: We consider how to resolve conflict effectively (#76), and we look at how to deal with bad behavior at work (#77). Then we look more widely at the phenomenon of office politics (#78) in terms of how it manifests itself, how you can mitigate it, and how to protect your team from it. Finally, we look at the particular challenge of individuals not doing well in their own role. We provide advice for handling poor performance (#79), and we consider the art of being tactful (#80).

76. Resolve Conflict Effectively (Fisher and Ury's Principled Negotiation)

As we discussed in the previous section (#75), conflict within a team can be upsetting for those involved, but it can also be positive – for example, when it involves discussing ideas that clash with one another and better ideas emerge as a result.

Using conflict to spark creativity is great in theory, but there is often a lot of emotion involved in these situations. If this isn't addressed as part of the process, people can get very upset with one another, and their working relationships can be irretrievably damaged.

This is where Roger Fisher and William Ury's principled negotiation is useful. Popularized in their book *Getting to Yes,* they suggest the following principles:

1. **Separate people from problems.** It is easy for a difference of opinion between people to become "personal." So, an important trick is to separate people and problems: You need to help your colleagues see that there are real and honest differences of opinion between them and that the other side is not just "being difficult."

2. **Listen carefully to people's different interests.** Instead of treating the discussion as a negotiation where people have established positions and need to compromise, treat it as a problem-solving process where you focus on people's interests – their needs, desires, concerns, and fears. Listen carefully

and honestly, without interrupting, and try to understand why the people in conflict think the way they do. Then "play this back" to them so that they know you understand where they're coming from. (You'll find that this mindful listening (#50) takes a lot of the emotion out of the situation and helps you understand their perspective.)

3. **Listen first, talk second.** If you are part of the conflict, you should talk about your own interests only when you've fully understood the other person's perspective and they've confirmed that understanding. As you do, keep your comments factual and focused on work-related issues, and try to use "I" statements rather than "you" statements so that no one feels attacked. Ask the other person to play their understanding of your interests back to you to confirm that they understand what you're saying.

4. **"Invent" options for mutual gain.** Now, without committing to any option, brainstorm a range of creative options that you could use to resolve the situation in such a way that both sides have their interests met and, ideally, gain in the process.

5. **Choose between options using objective criteria.** Finally, choose between the options you've explored using criteria that are as objective as possible. Make sure that the options chosen address people's interests appropriately but are also aligned with the team's and organization's mission.

Find out more about conflict resolution: http://mnd.tools/76

Source: Adapted from Fisher and Ury 1981.

77. Deal with Bad Behavior at Work

People get into conflict with one another for many reasons, and as we've seen, such conflicts sometimes lead to creativity and improved decision making. However, at other times, people can behave in a way that undermines the team and poisons the atmosphere. You need to take a firm line in such situations.

Unfortunately, it's often hard to tell if a behavior is genuinely wrong. For example, is it right for someone to turn up at work with extensive facial piercings? This may be fine in a creative marketing agency, but it may be deeply problematic for someone serving clients in a private bank. And is it okay for someone to yell at a colleague? Most people would say no, but in some work settings, this type of aggressive behavior is acceptable. So how do you decide what constitutes "bad behavior"?

There are some obvious tests: Is the behavior legal? Does it comply with organizational policies and procedures? And does it comply with professional or organizational codes of ethics? It's easy to know what to do in these cases, but you may not come across them often – most people know not to cross these lines, and your recruitment processes will hopefully "weed out" this type of rule breaker.

This leaves a whole lot of behaviors that don't fit with the normal rules, and it's often quite hard to know how to act in such circumstances. This is where the following tests can help:

Does the behavior support or harm the team's mission? Using our earlier example of facial piercings, there's a clear risk that these could repel the clients of the private bank, and as a manager, you'd need to act to avoid this. Customers of the marketing agency, however, may see piercings as evidence that it is tuned in to "youth culture," in which case they are not a problem.

Does the behavior promote or harm the cohesion of the team? Team members in the private bank may feel that facial piercings create a negative perception of their professionalism as a team, and this may cause conflict. In the marketing agency, piercings may just contribute to a cool, fun, creative atmosphere where people feel free to be open and be themselves.

Does the behavior cause unnecessary harm to the interests or safety of any individual member of the team? In the private bank, it may be acceptable for others to express their dislike of the team member's piercings, as long as it's done in a proportionate way and doesn't cross over into bullying. In the marketing agency, it's unlikely that anyone would complain in the first place.

> ## Tip
>
> You can end up in a difficult place if you allow your personal moral or religious beliefs to guide the way you judge good and bad behavior at work, particularly if these beliefs conflict with national employment law. **When at work, ensure that your judgments are made in a way that will stand legal scrutiny.** Consult with your HR team to make sure that you get decisions right, and keep appropriate records of what you've done and why.

Learn more about dealing with bad behavior at work: http://mnd.tools/77

78. Deal with Office Politics, and Protect Your Team from Them

Office politics refers to the way people manipulate others – for example, by gossiping and sharing confidential information to further their own personal objectives. Of course, there is always some of this going on, but a high level of office politics can be deeply corrosive within an organization. It's something that you need to be alert to so that you don't end up being undermined by it.

All of us do things at work that aren't strictly aligned with the organization's mission or our key objectives. Often these are small things – for example, social activities or personal favors that actually help our teams function more smoothly. We also need to be able to work effectively with senior and influential people around us and win resources for our teams, and this is where skills such as stakeholder management (#91), influencing skills (#94) and win-win negotiation (#100) become increasingly important as we climb the organizational ladder.

Some people see these types of activity as "political," but done in an open, honest way, they are a necessary part of functioning successfully within a complex organization.

Where this type of behavior becomes destructive, though, is when it focuses on the interests of individuals – often senior individuals – rather than on the interests of the people the organization is supposed to serve. In such circumstances, "rules" start getting broken, people get hurt unfairly, and decent treatment of people starts to break down.

People hate working in an environment like this. Gossip grapevines go crazy; people become cynical; goodwill, employee engagement, and creativity collapse; and the best people throw their hands in the air in exasperation and move on.

So, how can you deal with office politics in your team?

The answer lies with you, and it comes down to setting a good example (#49), leading in an inspiring, transformational way (#54), and making sure that people know how their work contributes to the organization's mission (#81 and 26.) If you do these things, then it's easy for everyone to apply the type of bad behavior at work tests we looked at in #77. Political behavior becomes obvious to everyone, and you can deal with it firmly and decisively.

And how can you protect your team if there is a lot of office politics going on around you? One answer is to ignore it and just get on with your job. But there is a risk that you and your team members lose out to colleagues who are actively engaging with politics. Another answer is to ditch the organization and move on to a better, less political place. The third and best approach is to try to do something about it. Running an employee survey with office politics questions is a good starting point (there is a perceptions of organizational politics scale that may be useful here; see the link below).

If you want to continue working in an organization and you can't change its culture, then you'll need to learn how to play the positive side of the political game and neutralize its negative side. To do this:

1. Identify the direct and indirect stakeholders in your work (we'll look at this in more detail in #91). These are the people who can impact the work you do positively or negatively, and you should be seeking to "manage" these people's views of what you and your team do.

2. Understand who strongly influences your most important stakeholders, and add these people to your list. You need to manage these people's views as well.

3. Build honest relationships with these people. Avoid empty flattery, and do what you can to build relationships based on trust and respect. Listen carefully to what they need from your team, deliver these things, and make sure they are aware of the good work that your people are doing.

4. Keep an eye out for "negative play," try to understand what is motivating it, and work out what to do to avoid it or neutralize its impact on you.

5. Be professional, positive, and polite; maintain your personal integrity; and – without being sanctimonious – uphold the team's and organization's mission and interests.

Tips

- ◆ Political behavior becomes particularly vicious when engaged in by people with narcissistic, Machiavellian, or psychopathic personality traits. Follow the link below to find out how to recognize dark triad behaviors such as these and to learn how to deal with them.

- ◆ By "playing a straight game," you may lose out on short-term, tactical opportunities; however, you'll preserve your reputation and self-respect. You can run into industry participants many times over the course of a career, and you will struggle to succeed in the future if you've damaged your reputation by playing politics.

Learn more about dealing with office politics: http://mnd.tools/78-1

Find out more about recognizing dark triad behaviors: http://mnd.tools/78-2

Find out more about the perceptions of organization politics scale: http://mnd.tools/78-3

79. Handle Poor Performance

Conflict and bad behavior are just two things that can go wrong within a team. Another is that people fail to perform effectively. Clearly, this is frustrating and difficult for you, and it causes problems for your customers. Moreover, it can put a lot of pressure on other members of your team, who may have to do unnecessary work to compensate for the poor performer. All of this means that you need to deal with performance issues promptly, rather than letting them fester.

Poor performance has two basic sources – low motivation and low ability. It may be obvious which of these you're dealing with. If it isn't, it may be best to assume you're dealing with both until you have good evidence one way or the other.

You can address low motivation by linking people's work to the organization's mission and by setting clear goals for them – we saw how you can do this when we looked at organizational missions and key results. You can set a good example for them, listen carefully to any problems they're experiencing, and structure their jobs to be as motivating as possible. We saw how to do this in Chapters 5 and 9.

You can also provide appropriate support (#59), feedback (#68), and coaching (#69) to help people improve their level of motivation. Bring all of this together into a clear performance improvement plan, document what performance levels you expect to see by what dates, and meet regularly to monitor how the plan is progressing.

You'll need to deal with ability issues using a different approach, and this is where the five Rs of performance improvement from David Whetten and Kim Cameron's book *Developing Management Skills* can help. The steps are:

1. **Resupply** – Here, you talk to people who are underperforming and make sure that they have the resources and support they need to do their jobs well. It's hard to do a good job if these aren't in place.
2. **Retrain** – Make sure people have the skills and training they need to do a good job. In many sectors, technology is changing quickly. Without knowing it, people can find themselves

with obsolete skills, and they can underperform as a result. Review the skills the underperformer needs, and provide appropriate training and development. (Skills matrices – see #67 – can help you evaluate this on a team-wide basis.)

3. **Refit** – If this doesn't work, look at the work the person is doing. Does he or she do a good job in some areas and a poor job in others? And can you change the person's role to focus on the former and minimize the latter without upsetting other team members? (Do this with aptitude issues. If people are lazy or lack self-discipline when doing boring or unpleasant jobs, you mustn't redistribute these to others – otherwise, you'll have a real crisis on your hands!)

4. **Reassign** – If the person is still struggling but he or she shows a good attitude to their work, you may need to move them into a different role where they can contribute effectively. This may involve demotion, which can be painful for all involved; however, it may be the right thing to do.

5. **Release** – If performance is still below an acceptable level after you've done all of this, then you'll need to let the person go. Otherwise, you're forcing other team members to "carry" the poor performer and you're showing that you're prepared to accept mediocrity, which will have a corrosive effect on team effectiveness.

Tip

When you're dealing with poor performance, involve your HR people right from the start. This is an area where it's easy to make mistakes with employment law, and these can cause serious problems for your organization.

Learn more about dealing with poor performance: http://mnd.tools/79

80. Be Tactful

So far in this chapter, we've explored how to deal with some diffi-cult but common management situations. You can manage these in a clumsy way or you can do them well, and this is where tact – the ability to communicate painful information sensitively – is important. If you prepare well and communicate your message tactfully, you've got a good chance of resolving the situation successfully. However, if you go in unprepared and blurt out the first thing that comes into your mind, you can make a difficult situation much worse.

So how can you deal with situations tactfully?

1. **Prepare appropriately.** Consider talking the situation through beforehand with an emotionally intelligent col-league – HR advisers are often the perfect people for this. Think about what the person you need to be talking to is likely to be thinking and feeling and what their points of sensitivity are likely to be. Try out the words you might use, explore the emotional impact they may have, and refine the message accordingly. Then consider how he or she may react and the different directions that your conversation may then go – you can prepare for these by role-playing different scenarios.

2. **Choose the right time to talk.** Find a time when the person you want to communicate with has time to talk, and be aware of the context – it may be best to delay your message if he or she is in the middle of dealing with highly emotional or difficult situations, for example.

3. **Choose your words carefully, and listen.** Be aware of the emotional impact of your words when you speak. Watch the other person's body language, and listen mindfully (#50) to the reply. If you're giving constructive criticism, remember to use "I" statements. For example, say, "I didn't understand what you were saying" rather than "You were unclear."

4. **Be aware of your body language.** Think about the mes-sages your own body language is giving, and make sure this

is consistent with your message. Psychologist Albert Mehra-bian famously discovered that when people are talking about feelings and attitudes, people understand as little as 7% of the message they receive from the words that people used, with 39% coming from tone of voice and 55% coming from facial expression. Make sure that you're "saying" what you mean to say with your body language!

5. **Manage your emotions.** If you find yourself getting angry or upset, give yourself time to calm down. Otherwise, you could find yourself saying something that you really regret!

Tip

Tact varies from culture to culture. In some countries, you need to be quite forthright in your feedback for people to take it to heart. In others, you need to be more sensitive. Judge your approach carefully, but don't be so tactful that you fail to get your message across.

Learn more about communicating tactfully, including getting tips on dealing with specific difficult situations: http://mnd.tools/80-1

Find out how to use role play to prepare for a difficult situation: http://mnd.tools/80-2

Learn more about how to read body language, and find out how to align your body language with your message: http://mnd.tools/80-3

Part IV

General Commercial Awareness

Chapter 15

Develop Situational Awareness

Although the techniques for being a great boss apply widely across different firms and industries, we don't want to suggest that there are any universal truths about how you should act. Good management is *situational,* which means that the right thing to do depends on the particular needs of the people we are managing and the specific circumstances we are facing. For example, you need to manage introverts and extroverts in a subtly different way, and your style of management in a crisis will be different from your style when times are good.

In this last part of the book, we therefore shift toward a more outward focus. We describe a range of tools and frameworks that help you navigate your way through the wider organization and the world beyond. If you have a good understanding of this external context, you will be able to make better choices in terms of how to focus your own attention and how to prioritize the time of your team members. You will also impress those above you, which can only be good for your longer-term career prospects.

This section is about improving your overall commercial and strategic awareness. We could put an entire book together on this topic, but in the interests of space, we focus on five particular techniques.

Every business needs a strategy, by which we mean an explicit set of choices about where and how to compete. Strategy is how a business translates its mission or purpose into practical operational choices. These choices then empower people across the organization to align their day-to-day work in a focused and efficient way.

The starting point in developing a strategy is to understand the organization's mission and values (#81), which clarify why it exists in the first place and what success looks like. The next step is to develop a point of view on the changing business environment, which is best done using the PESTLIED framework (#82). Devising a strategy then involves two further pieces of analysis. One is to understand customer needs, how competitors currently serve them, and what your business might do differently, which is a piece of analysis that is best done using value curves (#83). The other is to understand your organization's core competencies and how you can fully take advantage of these (#84). A useful way of bringing together and summarizing these external and internal perspectives is to use SWOT analysis (#85).

81. Understand Your Organization's Mission and Values (Mission Statements)

We have seen many times in this book how important it is for people to have meaning and purpose in their lives, and we have seen how you, as a manager, can provide meaning to others through the way you lead them.

Most organizations have some form of mission statement that reflects its guiding purpose – we quoted Ratan Tata, the patriarch of India's Tata Group, earlier when he called it a "spiritual and moral call to action." When mission statements are well crafted, they express why the organization exists – they provide guidance to employees and other stakeholders in terms of whom the organization serves and what it does to help these people. Such statements articulate the organization's "good character" to the outside world.

A mission statement is important not only as a statement to the outside world but also as a way of clarifying goals and priorities inside the organization. Everything that happens internally, as measured through formal goals and objectives, should be linked back to the broader mission. The mission ultimately guides the work that individuals do, it channels decision making and allocation of resources, and, as we saw in #77, it influences managers' judgment as to whether people's behaviors are right or wrong.

If you are in a senior executive role, you may find yourself involved in developing or refreshing your organization's mission statement. The process for doing this involves conversations with a wide variety of stakeholders – employees, customers, shareholders, suppliers, communities in which you work – so that you can understand how your organization is currently perceived. It then involves some brainstorming and discussion among a smaller group of senior people to develop an integrated point of view. Remember, a good mission statement should be grounded in reality (i.e. consistent with current views) but also aspirational (i.e. suggesting a desired future state that is better than today).

The outcome of this process is a simple summary statement, typically structured as a goal expressed in the first-person plural ("Our mission is to … "). Don't worry about making the wording elegant – it's more important that there is some real substance to the statement – for example, think of Google's desire to organize the world's information to make it universally accessible and useful or IKEA's mission to make a better everyday life for the many people.

Once the mission statement is in place, it is important that you as a manager understand how you (and your team) can contribute to delivering it. It's also important to understand the organization's values – the ways of doing things that people think are important – that underpin the mission. If you manage according to these values, you are likely to be seen as a good corporate citizen. What's more, if things go wrong as a result of following the mission honestly and applying these values, you have something of a defense that you can rely on.

If, however, you act in a way that goes against these things, whether deliberately or ignorantly, you can expect negative consequences. This will particularly be the case if something goes wrong as a result!

Tip

The best mission statements are concise and easy to remember. That way, people can hold them in their minds and use them to guide their everyday actions. Long, convoluted mission

> statements are difficult to use, they're likely to be forgotten,
> and they can show that the organization's leaders have failed
> to make tough choices.

Learn more about mission statements and how to create
them, including some example statements: http://mnd.tools/81-1

Find out more about business planning: http://mnd.tools/81-2

Find out more about values and how to identify them: http://mnd.tools/81-3

82. Scan for External Changes That May Impact Your Organization (PESTLIED Analysis)

A good mission statement has a timeless quality – it addresses some
sort of societal need that should still be valid decades from now. But
the business world is evolving very rapidly, and the choices your organization makes in terms of how it adapts while continuing to deliver
on its broader mission have to take these changes into account. This
is why you need to develop an awareness of the wider business world
beyond your organization's boundaries.

The acronym PESTLIED (political–economic–sociocultural–
technological–legal–international–environmental–demographic) is
very useful for this. It is a handy way of structuring your analysis of
the biggest drivers of change affecting the business world today, and
it helps you think about the most important changes that could affect
you in the future. To use PESTLIED, bring together people with a
good knowledge and experience of the organization and the outside
world, along with people with specialist knowledge of the relevant
domains. Then brainstorm (#48) the most important trends in each
of the PESTLIED areas:

Political – How is government policy evolving, and how is it
likely to change? Are levels of taxation, funding, or subsidy likely
to increase or decrease? Is the ethical or corporate social responsibility climate likely to change? When are your country's next
elections, and what is the outcome of these likely to be? And are
other political factors relevant?

Economic – How stable is the economy, and is it growing or contracting? What is happening to exchange rates, the supply of credit, and the price of commodities? How much disposable income do people or companies in your market have? How easy will it be to recruit a skilled workforce? And are other economic factors relevant?

Sociocultural – How are levels of education, health, and social mobility changing? How is technology impacting social change? How are attitudes to human rights, religion, politics, and culture changing? And are there other sociocultural factors that will affect your organization?

Technological – What new technologies are emerging that will impact your organization or your industry? What technologies are your competitors developing, and what patents are they registering? Are there technology hubs or educational or governmental programs you could align with? And are there other technological factors you should consider?

Legal – Are property rights and the rule of law secure? Are any proposed changes to law, standards, consumer protection legislation, employment rights, or business regulation likely to impact your organization? Are competition or monopoly rules likely to change? And are other legal factors relevant?

International – Are security alliances stable, or is there a threat of serious instability? What is happening with respect to regional trading blocs or political entities? What is likely to happen with respect to tariffs, sanctions, and the free flow of finance, goods, and services? And are other international factors changing?

Environmental – How are climate change, climate legislation, and renewable energy technologies likely to affect your organization? Is clean air or pollution likely to be an issue for your business or for technologies you use? Are there other environmental factors that are relevant?

Demographic – What shape is the country's population pyramid, how is this likely to change, and what does this mean? What is happening to immigration and emigration, and what ability is there to bring in foreign workers? What other demographic factors are relevant to your business?

Having done this brainstorming, you'll likely end up with several long lists of the changes going on around you. Bring these together into affinity groups (see the link to affinity diagrams below) and then prioritize your results to identify, say, the top 10 changes most likely to affect you.

Then, for each of these changes, ask, "So what does this mean for us?" several times over until you've explored its full potential consequences for your organization. Scenario analysis, which we looked at in #46, can also be very useful here.

Tip

Some of these headings will be relevant to you, and some won't be. Don't spend too much time with the less relevant areas; otherwise, you'll waste people's time and lose momentum.

Find out more about PESTLIED analysis and PEST analysis,
including seeing examples and downloading a template: http://mnd.tools/82-1

Find out how to use affinity diagrams: http://mnd.tools/82-2

Source: Adapted from Harding and Long 1998.

83. Understand How Companies Compete in Your Market (Value Curves)

At the heart of business strategy is the concept of differentiation – the idea that your business should offer a product or service that, compared to the offerings of your competitors, is sufficiently distinctive and valuable that customers will pay a premium for it.

There are many ways of analyzing competitive positioning. The one we recommend is called *value curves*, as described by W. Chan Kim and Renée Mauborgne in their 1997 *Harvard Business Review* article "Value Innovation: The Strategic Logic of High Growth."

Value curves help you understand the competitive factors that matter most in your market, how your competitors are addressing these, and what you can do to develop a distinctive offering (or unique sales proposition, USP) that your customers will value.

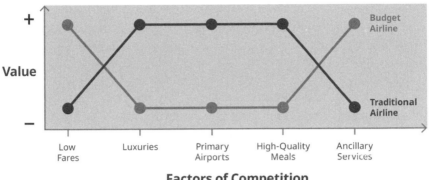

FIGURE 15.1   Value Curves for a Budget and Traditional Airline

USPs are important from a sales and marketing perspective for helping customers understand why they should buy your product, but they are also a key driver of business strategy in that they highlight capabilities that you need to focus on, defend, and enhance.

You can see an example of a value curve in Figure 15.1 showing competition between a budget airline and a traditional airline.

This shows the range of things that customers value on the horizontal axis and the extent to which a particular business delivers on these values on the vertical axis. In this example, the traditional airline offers a relatively luxurious service to its customers and flies into and out of convenient airports. By contrast, the budget airline is less convenient and offers a very basic service, but it does this very cheaply and then sells ancillary services as add-ons.

So, how can you use value curves to improve your business's competitive position? First, identify the key factors of competition, that is, the things that customers value, and then plot lines for your own company and for your key competitors. Then think about where you want to be. Start with where you are now, and ask yourself these questions:

◆ What factors can you reduce well below industry standards while still meeting the needs of a segment of your market? (See the link below for more information on segmentation.)

◆ What factors can be eliminated altogether?

◆ What new factors can be created or added that people in your market will value, thus making your product more attractive?

◆ What factors could you increase to enhance your competitive edge?

Even if you are not involved in decisions about strategy, it's important to understand the factors of competition in your industry and, in particular, the ones that your business is focusing on. This will affect the decisions you make and help you ensure that these are aligned with the overall strategy of your organization.

Tips

◆ We have described a process whereby company executives decide what factors are important, and they score how well the company and its competitors rate for each factor. It can also be useful to ask customers and potential customers for their perception of these things. This takes longer, but it gives you a clear, unbiased, outside-in view of how your organization compares with its competitors.

◆ It's useful to present the factors of competition on the horizontal axis in their approximate order of importance in the customer's purchase decision. This will help you make the right choices about which factors to change to get the biggest impact.

Find out more about value curves and how to use them:	http://mnd.tools/83-1
Learn more about market segmentation:	http://mnd.tools/83-2
Discover a wide range of other business strategy approaches:	http://mnd.tools/83-3

84. Understand Your Organization's Core Competencies

Although a clear understanding of customer needs and competitive positioning is central to a good business strategy, there is a third element that you should always take into account, namely the internal resources and capabilities of your organization.

A good understanding of your capabilities helps you figure out what you can actually deliver – for example, it makes no sense to position your organization as a high-end service provider if you have poorly trained and minimum wage employees. Understanding your capabilities can also help you define new products or services that might be developed in the future.

A useful way to think about this is to use the notion of *core competence,* developed by C.K. Prahalad and Gary Hamel in their classic 1990 paper "The Core Competence of the Corporation." The idea is that organizations should focus on improving the things that they do uniquely well and that are most valuable to customers – their core competencies – and should outsource the things they don't do so well to other organizations.

By doing this, a business will create distinctive products and services that command a premium position in the market and will avoid the "me too" world of commodity products that compete only on price.

So, what are the core competencies of your organization? You can probably come up with a long list of things that your company does well. Prahalad and Hamel offer three tests that you can use to separate "nice-to-have" capabilities from genuine core competencies:

1. **Breadth of application** – The core competence needs to be something that can be applied to many different markets or generate a range of potentially successful products. This breadth allows you to sustain growth beyond your initial market success.

2. **Relevance** – The competence needs to be valuable to customers in a direct or indirect way. Competencies often lose their significance over time. For example, many traditional retailers had competencies in store location and design, but these became increasingly irrelevant as online retailing took off.

3. **Difficulty of imitation** – The competence needs to be something that is hard for other organizations to imitate; otherwise, your advantage will be quickly eroded.

Often, you'll find that your most important competencies are actually bundles of related things rather than one narrow and specific thing. A well-known example is IKEA, which has developed a core competence in user-friendly furniture design through a combination of deep market knowledge, skilled designers, well-refined business processes, and strong relationships with component suppliers.

So, how can you use the idea of core competencies to improve your business and to advance your own career? Do the former by identifying competencies that will make the greatest positive difference to your organization's future and by looking for opportunities to develop them further.

From a personal career perspective, it pays to align your work and your self-development with your organization's core competencies. There's little point in becoming an in-house expert in an area that your company doesn't particularly care about (and may ultimately outsource) when you could use the same amount of effort to develop skills that help you succeed in a highly visible, business-critical area.

Find out more about core competencies and how to apply them: http://mnd.tools/84

Source: Adapted from Prahalad and Gary 1990.

85. Organizational Strengths, Weaknesses, Opportunities, and Threats (SWOT Analysis)

We looked at personal SWOT analysis in Chapter 1 as a great way of understanding your personal strengths and thinking about which career direction you should take.

It's also useful in an organizational context as a way of thinking about what your business does well and what sort of opportunities it should focus on and as a way of exploring weaknesses and countering the threats it faces. You can think of SWOT as a summary analysis of all the different elements that make up a business strategy. Strengths and weaknesses are linked to the resources and capabilities of the organization (#84), whereas opportunities and threats are linked to the external trends in the environment (#82) and the offerings of competitors (#83).

The fundamental approach is the same, whether you use SWOT analysis on a personal or an organizational level, so we won't repeat ourselves here. However, you need to ask slightly different questions at the organizational level of analysis:

Strengths – What does your organization do better than its competitors? What unique, highest-quality, or lowest-cost resources can you draw on that they can't? What core competencies (#84) do you have access to that they don't?

Weaknesses – Why do you lose sales to competitors? Where do they enjoy cost advantages that you don't have or access to resources that are not available to you? Where are customers unhappy with your offerings, and what do they complain about? And where do you struggle to deliver effectively? Now's the time to face any unpleasant truths so that you can do something about them.

Opportunities – When you look at your strengths, what good opportunities do these open to you? And what opportunities would arise if you could eliminate your weaknesses? What opportunities for growth do you see in your market that you are particularly well-placed to exploit? And what relevant changes in technology, societal trends, economic environment, or government policy can you see that create good opportunities (#82)?

Threats – What are your competitors doing that you should be worrying about? Are standards changing for your type of work, or are expectations of it increasing? And, as with opportunities, are there changes in technology, societal trends, economic environment, or government policy that could cause you problems?

If you're involved with setting strategy for your organization, SWOT analysis is often a useful starting point, and if you're a business, you can use it to understand your competitors as well as your own organization. Even if you are not involved at the strategic level, the insights from SWOT analysis will complement those you get by thinking about core competencies and value curves. This will help you make better decisions and keep your work aligned with where the organization is headed.

Tip

When you use SWOT analysis, it's easy to end up with a long, unfocused list under each of the SWOT headings, and this will not help you much. To get the best from the technique, accept only precise and, ideally, quantified statements; prioritize and prune ruthlessly so that you focus on only the most important factors; and apply it at the appropriate level – for example, at a product-line level rather than whole-company level.

Find out more about SWOT analysis, including seeing an
example and downloading a template: http://mnd.tools/85

Chapter 16

Get Ahead in the Wider Organization

I t's tempting to believe that doing a good job is enough to get you noticed – and promoted. Unfortunately, this is often not true.

Organizations are complex social structures where personal relationships matter and where good performance is multifaceted and somewhat subjective. They are also inherently competitive – there are fewer opportunities for promotion than there are qualified candidates, so you don't just have to be good; you have to better than others.

Another way to make the same point is to put yourself in your boss's shoes for a minute. She may have half a dozen other people reporting to her, she has deliverables and projects of her own, she is worried about her own career prospects, and she may have nonwork interests and distractions as well. How much attention does she actually pay to your individual performance and your career prospects? The answer is "Probably not as much as you would like." The onus, therefore, lies with you to build visibility and influence in the wider organization so that you get the opportunities you deserve.

Doing this isn't just about getting promoted. There is a second and equally important benefit, namely that many of the projects you are working on require coordination across departments. To be effective, you have to rely on others, and the more people know and value you, the easier it is to get their willing cooperation.

This section offers five techniques designed to help you work more effectively within the wider organization. The first is about understanding and shaping how others in your organization see you, using the PVI (perception, visibility, influence) model (#86). The other four focus in detail on different parts of the PVI model. To improve how others perceive you, it is useful to learn how to ask for feedback (#87) and to become better at building honest rapport with others (#88). Then there are two practical skills for broadening your influence: One is developing effective networking skills to improve your visibility (#89), and the other involves influencing your peers to get things done (#90).

86. Understand and Shape How Others in Your Organization See You (The PVI Model)

It's a sad truth that you can work hard, be good at your job, be a great team player – but still not get noticed. This can result in less well-qualified people being promoted ahead of you, which is obviously very upsetting.

It's tempting to put this down to office politics (#78), and sometimes you may be right to do so. However, it can also be that others are presenting themselves better in the workplace and, quite legitimately, developing more influence within the wider organization. Rather than just hoping to be noticed for their hard work, they've taken control of the situation and have done honest, straightforward things that help them stand out.

So how can you do this yourself? This is where the PVI model, developed by executive coach Joel Garfinkle, helps you get the recognition your talents deserve. PVI stands for three things – perception, visibility, and influence – that you need to address to get ahead:

Perception – This is about how others see you. There can be a wide gap between how you want to be seen and how people actually see you, and you need to make sure that you address this gap before you try to raise your profile in other ways.

Do this by making a list of the characteristics you want to be known for. Then ask for honest feedback on these points from your boss, your clients, your colleagues, and your friends (we look at a great technique for doing this next).

Where gaps exist between what you want and reality, set yourself SMART (specific, measurable, achievable, relevant, and time-bound) goals to close these gaps, and record these on your action program (#10).

Visibility – Once you're sure you'll be recognized for the right things, it's time to raise your profile. Remind yourself of the wonderful things you've done so that you can do this while still being authentic and feeling self-confident (#4).

Make sure your boss knows what you and your people have achieved. Send short progress reports when you've hit a key goal, or highlight the achievements of members of your team, gathering reflected visibility at the same time (the URL below gives more tips on this).

Networking (#89) is also important for increasing visibility. Try volunteering for challenging projects or relevant committees, cross-train people on key skills, and volunteer to do presentations on key projects to important stakeholders.

Influence – One important way to build influence is by becoming an expert in an area that matters to your organization. A good way to do this is through a growth mindset (#7): Take every step you can to build strong skills (see the link below), and reflect on and learn from the use of those skills, perhaps with journaling (#5) or with post-completion reviews (#31).

Another way to build influence is by developing high-quality connections across the organization. We discussed aspects of this in #63, and we'll discuss building rapport, alliances with peers, and wider networking later in this chapter. Finally, we'll explore at an elegant approach for influencing people when we look at the influence model (#94).

Learn more about the PVI model:	http://mnd.tools/86-1
Find out how to get the recognition you deserve:	http://mnd.tools/86-2
Discover ways to build strong skills and expertise:	http://mnd.tools/86-3

Source: Adapted from Garfinkle 2011. Reproduced with permission of John Wiley & Sons, Inc.

87. Ask for Feedback (The SKS Technique)

We saw the importance of managing how others perceive you in #86, and getting plenty of feedback is a key element of this technique – it helps you learn from the people around you, understand what is and isn't working for you, and adapt your approach accordingly. Without feedback, your learning will be much slower, and there will be things you don't know about that you can't address. Any performance problems will persist, and you may annoy people who are important to you without realizing it.

Managers often avoid giving feedback because it takes time, and it is hard to do well. Giving feedback also goes against cultural norms in many organizations and countries, and this, again, means you may get very little of it from your own manager.

This is where the SKS technique is useful. Credited to Phil Daniels of Brigham Young University, SKS refers to three questions you can ask of your manager or the people you're working with to invite feedback. These are:

◆ What should I stop doing?
◆ What should I keep on doing?
◆ What should I start doing?

The stop doing question highlights things you are doing wrong and allows you to take quick actions to get back on course. Make sure that you fully understand why these things are wrong, and then act on them right away!

The keep doing question shows what people appreciate about the way you work. It can also highlight talents you may not be aware of. Think about these carefully, and build on them.

The start doing question highlights gaps in what you are doing and areas where you can improve. Examine your emotions around these things to see if you are uneasy about them – perhaps because they go against your natural personality (#1), you're scared of doing them, or you're procrastinating (#13). In many cases, there are ways to overcome these barriers and take the necessary steps forward.

SKS is great because it's simple and it fits comfortably into regular meetings such as one-on-ones. If you actively ask for feedback like this, it makes it much easier for your boss to give it because it has been asked for and it needs little preparation.

As such, SKS puts you in control of getting feedback, and it allows you to make changes right away, rather than waiting many months for a formal review. It is also a way to get recognition for things you're doing well, which feels great, and it ensures your contribution is recognized.

Tip

Make sure you manage your emotions when you're using the SKS technique. Its purpose is to help people give you feedback quickly and easily, and you'll lose this benefit if you become "teary" when you receive negative feedback.

Find out more about the SKS technique: http://mnd.tools/87

Source: Adapted from Delong 2011. Reproduced with permission of Harvard Business Publishing.

88. Build Honest Rapport with Others

Another aspect of how others perceive you is the personal rapport you build with them. Researchers Linda Tickle-Degnen and Robert Rosenthal identified three things you share with someone when you feel that you have rapport with them:

Mutual attentiveness – You focus intensely on what the other person is saying or doing, and they do the same with you.

Positivity – You are warm and friendly to one another, and you enjoy one another's company.

Coordination – You are responsive to one another, and your body language and tone of voice move in sync.

Some of this comes naturally as we show dependability and trustworthiness with others and come to understand and trust them too. However, there is also some scope to actively develop rapport in an honest, nonmanipulative way.

Let's imagine you're going to meet someone for the first time. You want to start by getting the basics right, so you make a strong first impression by being well-groomed and by dressing appropriately – perhaps a little smarter than the person you're going to meet, but not too much so. Relax, smile, remember their name, and listen mindfully to what they say.

Next, try to find common ground. Get a conversation going with small talk (see the link below for more on this); ask open, unchallenging questions; and disclose harmless information about yourself, your interests, and your experiences.

Your aim is to try to find common experiences and interests with the other person. As you find these, explore them politely and non-controversially, and share your own thoughts about these situations. (If you're at an event, ask why they are attending or what they found interesting about a particular presentation; in other situations, you might ask where they went to college or what got them into their line of work.) Depending on the context, that may be all you want to do. Good relationships take a while to build, and you don't want to seem pushy.

However, at an appropriate time, you may want to find an experience to share. Perhaps buy this person coffee or lunch, or work together to solve a problem that matters to you both – perhaps your teams work together, and you can devise a process that people can use to interact effectively, or suchlike.

In time, you can build a strong relationship with this person, and this will stand you both in good stead for the future.

Tips

- When you're engaging in small talk, it can help to have a repertoire of small, appropriate stories that you can draw on. A little preparation can go a long way here!
- As a way of building rapport, some people recommend consciously mirroring people's body language, use of language, or speech patterns, such as tempo or tone of voice. Done naturally and well, this can help. However,

done crudely or with people who are "psychologically aware," this can be annoying, and it can break rapport and damage your reputation. Worse, it can be used to manipulate people, and that is just wrong.

Find out more about building rapport:	http://mnd.tools/88-1
Learn how to make small talk:	http://mnd.tools/88-2

Source: Adapted from Tickle-Degnen and Rosenthal 1990. Reproduced with permission of Taylor & Francis.

89. Develop Effective Networking Skills

Once people have healthy perceptions of you, the second stage in the PVI process is to increase your visibility. Networking effectively – both inside and outside your organization – will help you do this.

This sounds fine and obvious in principle; the benefits of networking in terms of expanding our sphere of contacts, developing opportunities, and building a positive image are undeniable. But many people see networking as cynical and self-centered, and they feel "dirtied" by it. As a result, they struggle with it.

You need to reflect on your own attitude toward networking. If you see it purely as a way of advancing your own career, then, yes, you are likely to approach it cynically, and it is unlikely to be effective. If, however, you approach networking as an opportunity to learn new things, meet interesting people, and uncover new opportunities, then you can be much more positive and successful in your approach.

So, how can you set yourself up to network effectively? These simple steps can help:

1. **Identify your networking objectives.** Think about what you want when you network. Do you want insights to help you work better? Do you want to get to know people in your wider organization? Do you want to understand your industry better? Or do you want to identify opportunities for your business? Make sure that your objective is positive and focused on the good of other people, not cynical and self-serving.

2. **Identify relevant events or networks.** Next, find the right activities to take part in to give you the greatest potential impact. For example, are there internal committees you can volunteer for, professional associations or chambers of commerce you can join, or networking events you can attend? Online groups are another option, but of course these virtual relationships tend to be quite shallow – you'll build the strongest relationships face to face.

3. **Think about what you can offer.** Successful networking is based on generosity and reciprocity – people will quickly see through you if you're just out for yourself. So think broadly about what you can offer that is interesting or of value while protecting your organization's confidentiality. (If you're new to an area, you may struggle with this, but you can at least be positive and appreciative of people's time, and that may be all that's needed.)

4. **Prepare.** Before each event, memorize a concise "elevator pitch" that says who you are and what you do (the link below will help you do this). Think about questions you can ask that will encourage people to open up, such as "So what do you like best about … " Practice answers to similar questions so that you can talk eloquently about the things that inspire you.

5. **Keep your objective in mind when you network.** When it comes to actual networking, here are a few tips to keep in mind.

    • In a crowded room, look for individuals standing alone or small, open groups of people chatting casually rather than closed groups of people talking intensely.

    • Focus on building a good relationship with people rather than grilling them to see if they'll be of benefit to you. Then, before you run out of things to talk about, close the conversation – you can ask for their card, for example, say what a pleasure it's been to speak, and then move on.

Learn more about networking effectively: http://mnd.tools/89-1
Find out how to prepare an elevator pitch: http://mnd.tools/89-2

90. Influence Your Peers to Get Things Done (Yukl and Tracey's Influencers)

The third part of the PVI model looks at influence, and this is particularly important when you're working with your peers, because you'll typically have no formal authority to insist that they comply with your requests.

There are good ways of influencing people and there are bad ways, and it's useful to understand the difference. This is where it helps to know about Gary Yukl and J. Bruce Tracey's 11 influence tactics, 6 of which are positive and 5 of which are negative.

The *positive* tactics don't harm your relationship when you use them. These are:

1. **Rational persuasion** – This involves using solid facts and logical arguments to make your argument; for example, you could put forward a well-researched business case for a marketing campaign that will benefit your business.

2. **Apprising** – Here, you explain how helping out will *indirectly* benefit the other person. For example, you might highlight how a coworker can raise her profile with the board by helping to make the campaign a success.

3. **Inspirational appeal** – This is about linking your idea to the values and ideals of the person you want to influence. Perhaps he cares deeply about environmental causes, and the product you want to promote has a positive environmental impact. By stressing this, you may be able to encourage him to contribute to the project.

4. **Consultation** – Here, you discuss your plan with key people before you firm it up so that they feel involved. Providing your consultation has been genuine and you've taken their views into account, this makes it more likely that they'll support it.

5. **Exchange** – This involves making an exchange – perhaps of your own time or some other necessary resource in return for the help of the other person. We'll look at this in more detail in #100 when we look at win-win negotiation.

6. Collaboration – Here, you do everything you sensibly can to make it easy for the other person to help you. In our example, you could do as much of the mundane and time-consuming part of the job as you can yourself so that they can do their part quickly and easily.

The *negative* tactics can leave people feeling manipulated, and this can damage your relationship with them. These are:

1. Legitimation – Here, you try to establish authority over the other person, perhaps by citing organizational rules and procedures. It is sometimes okay to use this approach, but it can lead to resentment or grudging compliance.

2. Coalition – This is where you "gang up" with others to push someone to take a course of action. This can leave the other person feeling bullied and that their opinion isn't valued.

3. Pressure – Here, you threaten someone, make strong demands, or continue to ask for something after they've said "no." This can make the other person feel stressed and angry, and they won't forget this.

4. Ingratiation – This involves trying to make people feel better about themselves before you ask them to do something. However, it often comes across as insincere. The other person is likely to disregard your warm comments and also feel cynical about your motives.

5. Personal appeals – You may ask someone to do something because of friendship, loyalty, or kindness. But there is a risk people will feel you are taking advantage of them – and they may expect favors in return that you don't want to give.

Find out more about Yukl and Tracey's influencers: http://mnd.tools/90

Source: Adapted from Yukl 2012. Reproduced with permission of Pearson Education, Inc.

Chapter 17

Make Change Happen in Your Organization

As companies grow and become successful, they build up large amounts of momentum – they hire people with particular skill sets and attitudes, they develop formal processes for sustaining a particular way of working, and they often focus on a fairly narrow set of measures of performance. But the competencies they build up over time can quickly become liabilities when there are major shifts in the business environment. In cases of mighty companies falling from grace, such as Nokia, Kodak, or Blockbuster, the story is always about executives failing to achieve the scale of change that was required. Typically, there is a good level of awareness of what is happening (for example, Kodak actually invented the digital camera and Nokia had touchscreen phones in prototype before the Apple iPhone was launched), but the challenge of fundamentally changing the structures, processes, and people in a large company is often too difficult.

The ability to manage change is, therefore, hugely important – and not just at senior executive levels. Midlevel managers have to be able to lead change programs within their areas of responsibility, and they also have to take an active role in large-scale change efforts. Most of the techniques in this book have been about working within a fairly clearly defined framework – even the techniques for creativity and innovation assumed a certain level of stability in the company as a whole. But in this chapter, we take a different approach and look at the various techniques needed to make major change happen.

By major change, we mean the sort of thing that makes many people uncomfortable, that has losers and winners, and that requires real leadership to help people make sense of it.

The starting point is to understand the stakeholders of your change program – who they are and what their needs are (#91). Then we discuss the key steps needed in a change process (#92) using Kotter's well-known eight-step guide. We describe a technique for understanding the emotional reactions of people as they go through a change process (#93). We also look at the tactics for persuading and influencing people effectively (#94).

These four techniques all assume you have a reasonable level of seniority and some formal authority over the people you are trying to take with you on a change process. The final technique is different – it is for managers at lower levels who are trying to lead change when they lack formal authority (#95).

91. Understand Stakeholder Needs, and Bring Stakeholders Along with You (Stakeholder Management and Power/Interest Grids)

We have all seen projects fail because of people issues. Money and energy are expended to make change happen, only for key people to reject it or for end-users to avoid using new tools given to them.

This often happens because the right individuals have not been consulted or informed about what is happening or they have not "bought in" to the need for the project. This is why stakeholder management is a vital part of change projects; and the larger the project and the more people it affects, the more important it is likely to be.

Stakeholders are the people who have an interest in the success or failure of a project and an ability to affect its outcome. They can be obvious groups such as employees and managers, but they can also be less obvious such as investors, governmental organizations, trade associations, trades unions, pressure groups, or the press.

Your boss	Shareholders	Government
Senior executives	Alliance partners	Trade associations
Coworkers	Suppliers	The press
Team members	Investors	Interest groups
Customers	Analysts	The public
Prospective customers	Future recruits	The community
Family	Key contributors	Key advisors

FIGURE 17.1   Possible Stakeholders in Your Change Project

To maximize the chance of success for your change project, it is wise to start managing stakeholders from the outset. To do this, follow these steps:

1. **Identify relevant stakeholders.** Brainstorm the people who are interested in your project and might be affected by its outcome. Figure 17.1 is a list of possible stakeholders.
2. **Assess their power, interest, and support.** For each stakeholder, assess how much influence they might have over your project, their level of interest, and whether they are likely to be positive or negative about it.

    Plot this analysis on a power/interest grid like in Figure 17.2. This helps make it clear where you need to focus your communication and your influencing efforts. It also shows you what approach you should use with different people.
3. **Plan how you'll "manage" your stakeholders.** For each significant stakeholder, think about their most important interests and issues, what support you want from them, and how you should work with them to win that support. (See our next tool, Kotter's eight-step change model, for more on this.)

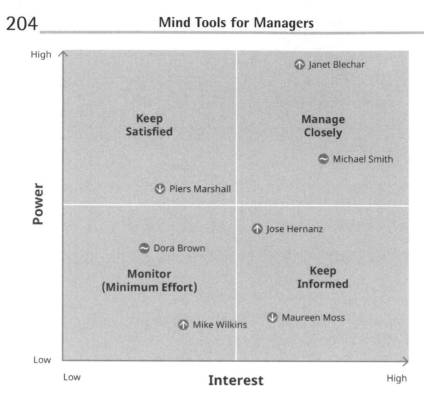

FIGURE 17.2 Example Change Project Power/Interest Grid

Tip

You may identify specific organizations as stakeholders. When it comes to communication, though, you need to find the right people within that organization to target. You need to manage stakeholder communication at an individual level, not an organizational level.

Find out more about stakeholder analysis, including using an interactive power/interest grid tool: http://mnd.tools/91-1

Learn how to manage stakeholders, including downloading a stakeholder management template: http://mnd.tools/91-2

Source: Adapted from Mendelow 1981.

92. Understand the Key Steps Needed to Succeed with a Change Process (Kotter's Eight-Step Change Model)

Once you've identified the most important stakeholders in your project, the next step is to communicate with them and "manage" them so that they support it enthusiastically. This is where John Kotter's eight-step change model can help you. Published in 1995, this model is based on lessons from more than 100 change projects. To use it, follow these steps:

1. **Establish a sense of urgency.** Look at your organization and your market situation, and communicate why it's important and urgent that this change go ahead.

2. **Form a powerful coalition.** Bring together a group of influential people with the power and enthusiasm to push the project forward (ideally, it should include many of the stakeholders you identified above – see #91).

3. **Create an inspiring vision for change.** We've seen the importance of vision many times in this book. Develop a short and motivating statement that encapsulates the desired future state of the organization (or one part of it) once the project has been implemented.

4. **Communicate the vision.** Don't just do this once and move on – communicate it at every opportunity, keep it fresh in people's minds, and discuss people's concerns openly and honestly with them.

5. **Empower others to act on the vision, and remove obstacles.** You cannot do everything yourself, so empower others to help build momentum, and do what you can to make it easier for them to support you.

6. **Plan for and create quick wins.** Demonstrate the potential success of your project by notching up some initial "wins" that show you are on track. This will help you build and sustain enthusiasm for the project.

7. **Consolidate improvements and build on change.** Some of the projects Kotter studied failed because managers "declared victory" too early and moved on, but the changes failed to take root, and their benefits gradually dissipated. To sustain change, you need to set fresh goals periodically and bring on new change leaders to maintain forward movement.

8. **Institutionalize new approaches.** Finally, for changes to stick, they need to become part of corporate culture. Continue "selling" the change project at every opportunity, celebrate people who support it, make sure that review and reward systems are aligned around the change, and ensure that new managers in key roles are natural champions of the new approach.

Learn more about Kotter's eight-step change process: http://mnd.tools/92

Source: Adapted from Kotter 1995. Reproduced with permission of Harvard Business Publishing.

93. Anticipate and Manage People's Emotional Reactions to Change (The Change Curve)

Kotter's eight-step change model is great for initiating and inspiring change, but it doesn't describe the emotions that people experience if they're affected by change but are not in control of it. These emotions can be intensely negative, and they can seriously undermine or stop a change project if you're not prepared for them.

This is where it helps to know about the change curve and to understand how to help the people affected by change through its stages. Often attributed to psychiatrist Elisabeth Kübler-Ross, it draws parallels with her work on personal transitions in grief. You can see an example of it in Figure 17.3.

Many people go through a predictable pattern of emotions as they experience unexpected change. In stage 1, they react with shock to the challenge to the status quo, and they may deny that the change is happening. In stage 2, as people start to experience the impact of change, they react with fear and anger, they may actively resist the change, and the organization may experience serious disruption to its performance as a result.

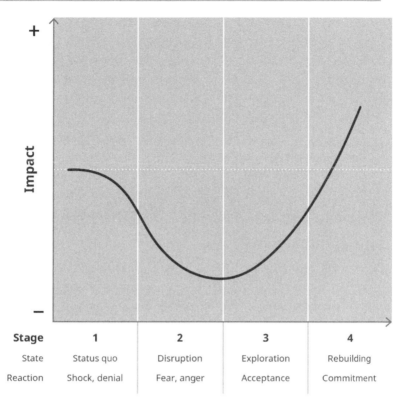

Stage	1	2	3	4
State	Status quo	Disruption	Exploration	Rebuilding
Reaction	Shock, denial	Fear, anger	Acceptance	Commitment

FIGURE 17.3   The Change Curve

Source: Kubler-Ross 1969. Reproduced with permission of Scribner, a division of Simon & Schuster, Inc.

If people successfully navigate stage 2, they may move to stage 3. Here, people let go and accept change, and they start exploring what it may mean to them and how they can adapt to it. Finally, in stage 4, they embrace change, and everyone reaps its benefits.

The trick with managing these stages is to anticipate them and help people adjust – this allows you to reduce the downside risks, shorten the length of time it takes to settle in, and increase your chances of success.

In stage 1, focus on providing information and answering questions without overwhelming people with details (if they're seriously upset, they may only be able to take a small amount of information in at any one time).

In stage 2, you need to be prepared to deal with anger. Anticipate objections and concerns, and do what you can to address issues honestly so that you can win people over. (We look at a useful tool for doing this next, in #94.)

In stage 3, provide plenty of training and support for people to try out new approaches and explore the opportunities that change will bring. And in stage 4, celebrate the success of the project, and make sure that everyone's contribution is fairly and properly recognized.

Learn more about using the change curve: http://mnd.tools/93

---

94. Persuade and Influence People Effectively (The Influence Model)

It's all very well and good for us to talk about persuading people to support your change project, but this can be very hard to do, particularly if people feel threatened by it and become angry as a result.

This is where the influence model can help you. Published in 2006 by researchers Allan Cohen and David Bradford, it draws on the principle of reciprocity – i.e., fair exchange – to win people over. It's particularly useful where they don't support you, where you have a poor or nonexistent relationship with them, or where you've run out of other ways of trying to persuade them to help you. To use it, follow these steps:

1. **Assume that everyone is a potential ally.** Even if you've had no success getting the other person to cooperate, start with the presumption that they will come around if you work at it. If you assume that the other person is hostile and you act accordingly, all you'll do is trigger hostile behavior in return.

2. **Clarify your own goals and priorities.** Be absolutely clear what you want from the other person. Prioritize your goals so you know what to focus on, and separate real objectives from "being right" or "having the last word."

3. **Understand your potential ally's world.** Try to understand what the other person cares about and what pressures they are under. A good way of doing this is to ask the

person directly. If this isn't possible, try to put yourself in their shoes – for example, in terms of what their boss is demanding from them, how they are being measured or rewarded, and what it will cost them to agree to what you want.

4. **Identify relevant "currencies" – the ally's and yours.** Think about what matters to your potential ally – whether this is money, prestige, being liked, or something else. Then think about the resources you have available, whether concrete objects such as money or supplies or less concrete resources such as help, emotional support, meaning, connections, or respect from people who matter to them.

5. **Approach the person in the right way.** Start by thinking about the relationship you have with the person already; this will influence how you make your approach. Then think about their preferred style for receiving information – for example, in a face-to-face meeting, over lunch, or by e-mail. Listen carefully to what they want, and deal with them in a way that they're comfortable with.

6. **Make the exchange.** Once you know what the other person wants and you know what you have to exchange, you can make an appropriate offer (we'll look at win-win negotiation in #100). Do this in a way that builds trust – after all, you may have to deal with them again in the future. Show empathy and respect for the other person, and express gratitude for their help.

Tip

We looked at Yukl and Tracey's Influencers in Chapter 16 (#90), and we'll visit the topic of influence again in Chapter 18 when we discuss negotiation. These tools work well together – mix and match approaches to suit the situation.

Learn more about the influence model, including seeing an
example of it in action: http://mnd.tools/94

Source: Adapted from Cohen and Bradford 2005. Reproduced with permission of John Wiley & Sons, Inc.

95. Lead Change Without Formal Authority ("Stealth Innovation")

It's not just people affected by change you need to persuade – sometimes you need to win over conservative senior managers who may not be prepared to fund the work needed to prove an idea. One way of doing this is to develop your idea quietly, behind the scenes, and prove success early on without getting prior approval.

This is particularly useful where ideas are radical and potentially disruptive internally, where they need more work to be fully shaped, and where they might end up being shot down by senior managers before they have a chance to prove themselves. (This is important because once an idea has been rejected by busy senior stakeholders, it can easily stay rejected, even if problems have been overcome and the idea has been significantly improved.)

This is where the notion of *stealth innovation,* as described by Paddy Miller and Thomas Wedell-Wedellsborg in a 2013 *Harvard Business Review* article, is useful. According to these researchers, to do this well, you need to:

1. **Get the support of midlevel managers.** Build a network of support for your idea among accessible managers who can help you make the project succeed. Pick people who trust and like you. Ask for their advice, and shape the project accordingly.

2. **Prove the value of your idea.** Build an inexpensive, working prototype of the product or service (ideally using spare time and borrowed or self-purchased resources), and test it out on a small, low-risk group of real users to see what they think of it. (See the design thinking tool – #44 – for more on this.) The idea here is to gather robust data showing that the idea is a success. Of course, if the data turns out negative, you can always abandon the idea at this stage, while it's still under the radar and little is at stake.

3. **Beg, borrow, or scavenge for the resources you need.** It's unlikely that you'll get a budget for a stealth project – so use your wits to access the resources you need. Tap into your network of contacts to borrow unused equipment, access

spare or surplus resources, barter resources you have for ones you need, or beg a few hours of time from people with key expertise.

4. **Have a communication plan.** Know what you'll say and how you'll manage the situation if your project attracts senior-level attention before you're ready for it. Miller and Wedell-Wedellsborg recommend aligning it with existing projects or strategic priorities, many of which have indistinct boundaries. Another approach is to say you're doing research for a proposal that you'll make to senior managers when you've tested the idea properly.

At some point, your stealth project will need to be put forward in a formal way for senior management buy-in and funding, but if you have taken the steps above, your chances of success will be significantly greater.

Tip

Be very careful not to disrupt existing programs when you use this approach. Resources can be scarce within an organization, and senior managers may have fought tough battles to get their programs funded and underway. You can expect trouble if your stealth innovation work slows delivery of these projects!

Learn more about stealth innovation: http://mnd.tools/95

Source: Adapted from Miller and Wedell-Wedellsborg 2013. Reproduced with permission of Harvard Business Publishing.

Chapter 18

Work Effectively with Customers and External Stakeholders

Although the biggest part of a manager's job tends to be internally focused (i.e. enabling others to get things done), it is vital to retain a certain level of external focus and, more specifically, to keep an eye on the ultimate customer or user of your company's products and services. If you are a manager working in sales, marketing, or customer service, you will do this as a matter of course. But keeping the customer in mind is also important for managers working in factories, supply chains, and administrative support functions. For example, many pharmaceutical companies make a point of inviting patients and doctors to speak to people working in back-office roles such as finance or support. This helps to remind those people why the company exists and what needs they are ultimately addressing. Studies have shown how this type of customer interaction helps employees to stay motivated and make better decisions about where to focus their efforts.

This final chapter provides some techniques and frameworks to help you understand and work effectively with customers and build relationships with a wide variety of external stakeholders.

We start with two specific techniques for making sense of customers. One is to understand your customer's worldview (#96) by creating personas that represent particular customer segments. The other is understanding and developing your relationship with your customers (#97) by mapping out how they experience your product or service in practice.

212

We then move deeper into the particular techniques you use for selling and negotiating with customers. First, we help you understand how decisions are made in another organization (#98) so that you can find the right people to speak to and influence. Then we look at the challenges of negotiating, first looking at the particular approach you should take in a given negotiation (#99) and then analyzing how to work with the other party to create a mutually beneficial outcome in the negotiation (#100).

96. Understand Your Customer's Worldview (Develop Customer Personas)

To serve your customers effectively, you need to understand who they are and how they see the world, so that you can design your products and services around their needs. We saw how important this is when we looked at design thinking (#44) and ethnographic research (#45).

If you are running a small business, it is relatively easy to take a customer-focused approach, because you are typically meeting with customers and prospective customers on a daily basis and you are confronted with their unique problems and challenges. But as your business scales up and you become more detached from day-to-day selling, there is a risk that you start viewing customers in a generic or homogeneous way. The result is that your communications can end up being inconsistent, dull, and off-target.

This is where it helps to develop a persona that represents a typical member of your audience. This is a short, research-based portrait of a typical customer, written up as if he or she were a real person with a name, a face, a personality, a back story, attitudes, likes and dislikes, and problems that he or she needs to solve.

By having this persona in your mind when you're communicating with your audience, you can empathize more closely with the circumstances and needs of people you're addressing, and give them better service as a result.

So how can you develop a persona? Start by analyzing the demographics of the customer group you want to serve. Begin with gender, age, location, and occupation information from customer survey data, and base your persona around the most frequent values for these.

If you have data for marital status, family role and composition, salary, and education, use that; otherwise, research typical values.

Then interview customers who match the profile of the persona – at least 5 and as many as 30, if you have the resources. Ask general questions about the person's life and work goals, their background and interests, key events that have shaped the way they think, their values and fears, their frustrations, the patterns of their everyday life, and the media they consume so you can get a rounded picture of them.

Then zoom in on how they use your product or service. How did they encounter it? What did they think as they went through the purchase process? What do they like about it, and what would they change if they could?

Pull all this information together on a single sheet of paper. Choose an image from a stock photo library that represents the customers you have talked to and come up with a name for the person. Add in demographic information, and come up with a tagline that sums this person up. Write a background piece based on your research. Do everything you can to bring your persona together as a human being you can identify with and empathize with.

The next time you're thinking about marketing to this customer group, hold this persona in your mind and design your offering around it. You'll be much more interesting and relevant to your audience if you do!

Tip

You can address your customers as a single audience with a single persona, but this one-size-fits-all approach will suit some people but not others. It's often better to break your audience down into segments – groups of individuals with common characteristics and needs (see the URL below). Each customer segment should be represented by a different persona.

Find out more about developing personas, including seeing an example: http://mnd.tools/96-1

Learn more about market segmentation: http://mnd.tools/96-2

97. Understand and Develop Your Relationship with Your Customer (Customer Experience Mapping)

Once you have insight into who your customers are, it's important to understand how they interact with your organization so that they can have the best possible experience. In a world where customer reviews and star ratings shape what we buy, this notion of "delighting" the customer is important.

The problem is that organizations are often complex, with many different teams having an impact on the customer's experience and each providing specialized parts of the service. Even if some teams do their jobs efficiently, problems with poor handovers often result in an unsatisfactory experience for customers.

Customer experience mapping helps you look at the service you offer from your customers' perspective. It helps you deliver a well-integrated, seamless experience that delights them. There is a brief example in Figure 18.1.

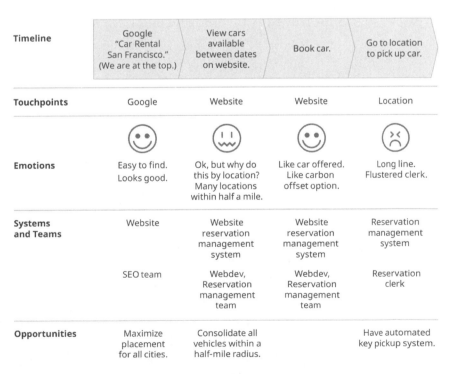

Timeline	Google "Car Rental San Francisco." (We are at the top.)	View cars available between dates on website.	Book car.	Go to location to pick up car.
Touchpoints	Google	Website	Website	Location
Emotions	Easy to find. Looks good.	Ok, but why do this by location? Many locations within half a mile.	Like car offered. Like carbon offset option.	Long line. Flustered clerk.
Systems and Teams	Website	Website reservation management system	Website reservation management system	Reservation management system
	SEO team	Webdev, Reservation management team	Webdev, Reservation management team	Reservation clerk
Opportunities	Maximize placement for all cities.	Consolidate all vehicles within a half-mile radius.		Have automated key pickup system.

FIGURE 18.1   A Sample Customer Experience Map

There are many different approaches to customer experience mapping – we provide a link to a gallery of different formats below. (Note that a customer *journey* map is essentially the same thing as a customer *experience* map.) Often the customer experience is shown using a series of "swim lanes" running horizontally across a page. Individual swim lanes show the following:

- A **timeline** showing the individual steps that customers go through to purchase and use your product or service.
- The **touchpoints** where customers interact with your organization at each stage of their experience.
- An indicator – often an emoji – showing the **emotions** experienced by customers at each step.

Customer experience maps can also have additional swim lanes, such as:

- A list of **internal teams and systems** involved at each stage. These can be split between "front of house" and "backstage" elements.
- A list of **opportunities for improvement** at each stage.

Your customer experience map should ideally be created by a combination of frontline people delivering the service to the customer (who will be aware of the full complexities involved at each stage) and real users (who will be aware of the experience and frustrations of using the service). Once you've drawn up your map, ask yourself these questions:

- Does the process make sense and flow in an efficient, easy-to-follow way? Or could you rearrange things so that it does?
- Is each stage strictly necessary, or is it caused by flaws in your internal structures? For example, would you need to move customers between teams if information was more readily available? And do you really need an account number (which the customer can't be expected to know) at each stage, or can other, known identifiers be used?

♦ What are your customers' most common frustrations and issues at each stage? For example, are you asking for the same details several times over? Are you providing appropriate confirmation that key actions have been taken?

Tip

It's possible to have high levels of customer satisfaction across individual touchpoints and still end up with dissatisfied customers because the overall "customer journey" is cumbersome or confusing. So, in addition to ensuring that each interaction is handled well, make sure that the whole journey makes sense from the customer's perspective.

Find out more about customer experience mapping: http://mnd.tools/97-1

See a gallery of different formats that you can use for your
customer experience/journey maps: http://mnd.tools/97-2

---

98. Understand How Decisions Are Made in Another Organization (Influence Mapping)

Although star ratings and reviews influence a lot of purchase decisions for consumer goods, the purchase process for business-to-business products can be very different, and many different people within a client organization can contribute to it. Many inexperienced salespeople have encountered the heart-sinking situation where they think they've made a sale only to find that the decision needs to be signed off by the person's boss, by purchasing, by IT, and so on across the organization.

But this isn't just confined to situations where you're trying to make a sale. Whole networks of people influence almost any major decision in one way or another, and you may need to satisfy all of these people to get the decision you want.

You can use a technique called *influence mapping* to understand who the key decision makers are for this type of situation, along

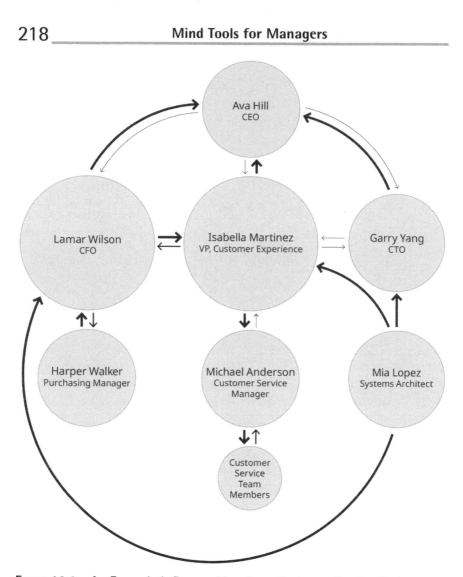

FIGURE 18.2   **An Example Influence Map for a Customer Service Systems Purchase Decision**

with the network of people who influence them. Figure 18.2 shows an influence map for a typical customer service system purchase decision.

Here, the circle size shows the person's influence over the decision. Arrows and the direction of arrows show the influence relationships that exist; the weight of arrows show the strength of these relationships.

In this example, the salesperson has been dealing with the customer service manager, Michael Anderson, up to this point. Michael and his team like the new system. What the diagram shows, though, is that Michael isn't the real decision maker.

Ava Hill, the CEO, and Garry Yang, the CTO, have the power to stop the contract if they are not happy with it, but they aren't particularly interested in the project – they have other things to think about, and they're both content to let their subordinates decide.

Isabella Martinez, Michael's boss and the VP of customer experience, is a key decision maker, and she needs to coordinate the rest of the organization to sign off on his new system. She has a great relationship with Mia Lopez, the systems architect, and values her technical opinion. She has a weaker relationship with Lamar Wilson, the CFO, but needs his agreement to sign off on the contract.

Lamar is the other key decision maker. He likes Isabella, but his job is to ensure that the agreement makes sense from a financial and commercial perspective. He has delegated a lot of the details to Harper Walker, the purchasing manager, whose view he trusts. He also has a lot of respect for Mia's technical insights.

What this means is that the salesperson needs to secure the agreement of Mia Lopez, Harper Walker, Lamar Wilson, and Isabella Martinez before the deal can go ahead – she has a lot more work ahead of her to figure this out and to give them the information they need to be happy, so that she can close the sale.

This example shows the sort of work you may need to do to get agreement on something from an external organization. However, this approach works just as well with parts of your own organization that you do not intuitively understand – as such, it can be a useful technique for general project management and change management (see the stakeholder analysis approach we described in #91).

Learn more about influence mapping: http://mnd.tools/98

99. Decide the Best Approach to a Negotiation (Lewicki and Hiam's Negotiation Matrix)

Negotiation is a key part of the purchasing process, particularly for expensive items such as the customer service system we used as an example in #98. People often worry about the approach they should take to negotiation: Should they play hardball and try to get the very best deal for themselves and their organization, or should they adopt a more consensual, win-win approach that works well for both sides?

The answer is that it depends on the situation, and that's where Roy Lewicki and Alexander Hiam's negotiation matrix, published in their book *Mastering Business Negotiation,* can help you think about the best approach to take (See Figure 18.3).

This matrix shows the importance of the outcome to you on the horizontal axis and the long-term importance of the relationship to you on the vertical axis. The simple logic here is that you shouldn't waste effort where the outcome of the negotiation doesn't matter to you much, and you can be much more demanding where you don't expect to have a long-term relationship with the other person.

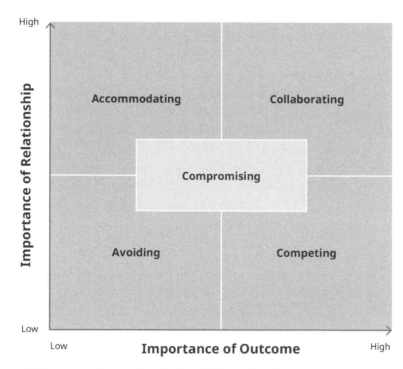

FIGURE 18.3   **Lewicki and Hiam's Negotiation Matrix**

Source: Lewicki and Hiam 2010. Reproduced with permission of John Wiley & Sons, Inc.

The different areas of the matrix show the strategies you should use in the different situations:

Avoiding (low importance of outcome, little ongoing relationship) – Don't waste time on the negotiation. Either back out of it, or accept the other person's conditions and move on.

Accommodating (low importance of outcome, important ongoing relationship) – Again, don't waste too much time on the negotiation. Make a token show of resistance so that people don't think you're a pushover in future negotiations, but broadly accept the other person's offer and maximize the goodwill you get by doing this. ("Because it's you, we'll go with this.")

Compromising (medium importance of outcome, medium importance of ongoing relationship) – Here, it isn't worth putting in the time to craft an elaborate agreement; you want some improvement in the outcome, and you need some ongoing relationship with the other person. Often, the quickest approach in this situation is to know what you want, understand what the other person wants, and meet them halfway.

Competing (important outcome, low importance of ongoing relationship) – This is where you might want to play hardball. You don't expect to deal with the other person again, and you want the best possible deal. Be tough, and if the other person doesn't expect to deal with you again, assume that he or she will be equally tough. (As an individual, you can expect this type of negotiation when you buy a house or a car.)

Collaborating (important outcome, important ongoing relationship) – Here, you need to get a good result, and you want a strong, ongoing relationship with the other person. Your approach to negotiation should focus on working together to identify and create opportunities for you both to get what you want out of the negotiation – and any future relationship. We'll look at how you can do this next when we look at win-win negotiation (#100).

Tips

◆ Just as you use this model, the other person is likely to be using it as well, whether consciously or intuitively. Before you start negotiating, look at the situation from their perspective, think about the strategy that they are likely to use, and adapt your approach appropriately.

◆ When you're in a competing situation, keep your own personal sense of ethics in mind. Make sure that you don't take any action that damages your reputation, but also be firm about what you want. Be aware that the other person may have a weaker sense of ethics than you have, and guard against any inappropriate behavior.

Find out more about Lewicki and Hiam's negotiation matrix:　　http://mnd.tools/99-1

Learn about distributive bargaining, an approach you can use in the compromising and competing areas of the negotiation matrix:　　http://mnd.tools/99-2

100. Collaborate to Create Mutually Beneficial Outcomes (Win-Win Negotiation)

There are many situations (as we saw in #99) where you need to take a collaborative approach to negotiation – you are looking for a successful outcome, but you also want to maintain a strong ongoing relationship with the other person. This is where win-win negotiation is a great technique to use.

The starting point is to prepare thoroughly. Think about these things:

Goals – What precisely do you want out of the negotiation? And what do you think the other person wants? (Bear in mind that you may be wrong about this, and you'll need to confirm this one way or the other when you negotiate.)

Relationships – Is there a prior relationship – good or bad – between yourself and the other person? If so, what should you do about this to make sure that the negotiation succeeds? If not, how will you build a working relationship?

Power – Who has the most power in the negotiation? Who controls scarce resources, and who stands to lose the least if no agreement is reached?

BATNA – What is the *best alternative to a negotiated agreement* that you and the other person have? This is your fallback position if you can't come to an agreement, and if it is particularly unattractive, you will likely need to compromise much more in the negotiation.

Trades – What do you each have that the other person wants but that you're comfortable to give away to get the deal you want?

Possible solutions – Based on all of this, what possible compromises or improved outcomes for both sides could there be?

When it comes to conducting the negotiation, the process of win-win negotiation is very similar to the principled negotiation approach we looked at in #76. Indeed, you can argue that conflict resolution is just a special case of win-win negotiation. The steps of this process are: Make relationships a priority, separate people from problems, listen carefully to people's interests, listen before you speak, invent options for mutual gain, and choose between options using objective criteria.

The most important of these steps is where you invent options for mutual gain. Spend plenty of time doing this, and you could end up with results that delight both of you!

Tip

BATNAs are important, and it's worth spending some time thinking about them when you're preparing for your negotiation. Do the following:

1. List the alternative actions you might take if you can't reach an agreement.

2. Improve the most promising actions, and develop them into practical options.
3. Select the best option. This is your BATNA.
4. Then think about what the other person's BATNA might be. They may or may not be clear about this, but having an idea about this will help you avoid making an unrealistic offer.

Find out more about win-win negotiation, including
downloading a preparation template: http://mnd.tools/100

Appendix

Survey Methodology

More than 15,000 managers across the world contributed to this book. They provided us with their views on the most important tools and techniques in each area of management, and this helped us to make the final selection of tools that appear in it. This appendix provides some additional information on the methodology we used.

The first step was to draw up a long list of tools. The MindTools.com website lists more than 1,000 tools, frameworks, and concepts, so this was our starting point. As we began to categorize the tools, the three concentric circles (manage yourself, manage others, manage the wider context) emerged as a simple organizing framework, and each circle was then further broken down into coherent elements, giving us the 18 chapters that constitute the book.

For each chapter, we put together a long list of 10 to 12 tools, based on our own judgment and analysis, as well as their popularity on the MindTools.com website. For the online survey, we asked respondents to identity the top five most important tools from this list. This was an important point in our survey design. We could have asked respondents to evaluate each tool on a 1–7 scale, but this approach typically leads to similar ratings across the board (i.e. all the tools are deemed important). Our design was a way to force people to make choices – to say that tool X is more important than tool Y.

The sample of managers we sent the survey to were users of MindTools.com. The full-length survey would have taken about 40 minutes to complete, so we split it into thirds. Some people

TABLE **A.1**   **Survey Respondents**

Total Respondents	15,242
Gender Split	57% female
	43% male
Age Split	21% <36 years
	56% 36–55 years
	22% >55 years
Most Represented Nationalities	32% US
	13% UK
	8% Australia
	6% India

got one set of questions; others got the other sets. In total, we sent the survey to approximately 850,000 people, and we received 15,242 responses. Table A.1 provides a rough breakdown of the nationalities, ages, experiences, and genders of the respondents.

For each chapter in the book, we ended up with a ranking of tools, and you can see these rankings using the URL below. A score of 70% means that of all the respondents to the survey, 70% of them chose that tool in their top five. As a general rule, we chose the top five or six tools in each category to feature in the book. There were two cases where we used our judgment in promoting one particular tool ahead of another because we felt it was sufficiently important. For example, agile project management has boomed in recent years, and we felt it needed to be included, even though many of our survey respondents did not include it in their top five. We also added in the key idea of transformational leadership, which we had not included in the survey.

View the results of the "Mind Tools for Managers" survey, showing which tools and concepts made the cut for this book and those that did not, across our 18 domains of management: http://mnd.tools/A1

References

M any MindTools.com articles were referred to in the writing of this book. Links to these are shown at the bottom of each tool, so we do not repeat them here.

Ale, B. and Slater, D. (2012). Risk matrix basics. http://riskarticles.com/wp-content/uploads/2012/09/Risk-Matrices-The-Basics-David-Slater.pdf (accessed 18 August 2017).

Allen, J., Dunn, A., Scott, C. et al. (2015). Implementing after-action review systems in organizations. In: *Cambridge Handbook of Meeting Science* (eds. J.A. Allen, N. Lehmann-Willenbrock, and S.G. Rogelberg). Cambridge University Press.

Anderson, K. (2009). Ethnographic research: A key to strategy. *Harvard Business Review*, March 2009.

Aven, T., Andersen, H.B., Cox, T. et al. (2015). Risk analysis foundations. *Society of Risk Analysis*. http://www.sra.org/sites/default/files/pdf/FoundationsMay7-2015-sent-x.pdf (accessed 31 December 2017).

Bandura, A. (1971). *Social Learning Theory*. General Learning Press.

Bandura, A. (1992). Exercise of personal agency through the self-efficacy mechanism. In: *Self-Efficacy: Thought Control of Action* (ed. R. Schwarzer). Routledge/Taylor & Francis Group.

Bartos, O.J. (1995). Modelling distributive and integrative negotiations. *The Annals of the American Academy of Political and Social Science* 542(1).

Bass, B.M. (1996). *A New Paradigm for Leadership: An Inquiry into Transformational Leadership*. U.S. Army Research Institute for the Behavioral and Social Sciences.

Baumeister, R.F., Campbell, J.D., and Krueger, J.I. (2003). Does high self-esteem cause better performance, interpersonal success, happiness, or healthier lifestyles? *Psychology Science in the Public Interest* 4.

Beck, J.S. (1995). *Cognitive Therapy: Basics and Beyond*. Guilford Press.

Birkinshaw, J. (2013). *Becoming a Better Boss*. Jossey-Bass.

Birkinshaw, J.M. and Cohen, J. (2013). Make time for the work that matters. *Harvard Business Review*, September 2013.

Bligh, M.C. and Kohles, J.C. (2013). Do I trust you to lead the way? In: *The Wiley-Blackwell Handbook of the Psychology of Leadership, Change and Organizational Development* (eds. L.H. Skipton, R. Lewis, A.M. Freedman et al). Wiley Blackwell.

Brown, T. (2008). Design thinking. *Harvard Business Review*, June 2008.

Brugha, R. and Varvasovszky, Z. (2000). Stakeholder analysis: A review. *Health Policy and Planning* 15(3).

Casciaro, T., Gino, F., and Kouchaki, M. (2016). Learn to love networking. *Harvard Business Review*, May 2016.

Chan Kim, W. and Mauborgne, R. (1997). Value innovation: The strategic logic of high growth. *Harvard Business Review*, January–February 1997.

Chan Kim, W. and Mauborgne, R. (1999). Creating new market space. *Harvard Business Review*, January–February 1999.

Chao, G.T., Walz, P., and Gardner, P.D. (1992). Formal and informal mentorships: A comparison on mentoring functions and contrast with non-mentored counterparts. *Personnel Psychology* 45(3).

Cherian, J. and Jacob, J. (2013). Impact of self efficacy on motivation and performance of employees. *International Journal of Business and Management* 8(14).

Cohen, A.R. and Bradford, D.L. (2005). The influence model: Using reciprocity and exchange to get what you need. *Global Business and Organizational Excellence* 25(1).

Cohn, M. (2017). Sprint retrospectives. https://www.mountaingoatsoftware.com/agile/scrum/meetings/sprint-retrospective (accessed 4 August 2017).

Corbett, M. (2015). From law to folklore: Work stress and the Yerkes-Dodson law. *Journal of Managerial Psychology* 30.

Cotman, C.W. and Berchtold, N.C. (2002). Exercise: A behavioral intervention to enhance brain health and plasticity. *Trends in Neurosciences* 25(6).

Csikszentmihalyi, M. (1990). *Flow: The Psychology of Optimal Experience*. Harper and Row.

Cutlip, S.M. and Center, A.H. (1952). *Effective Public Relations: Pathways to Public Favour*. Prentice Hall.

DeLong, T.J. (2011). Three questions for effective feedback. *Harvard Business Review*, August 2011.

Devendra, R. (2014). Key elements of the sprint retrospective. https://www.scrumalliance.org/community/articles/2014/april/key-elements-of-sprint-retrospective (accessed 4 August 2017).

Diehl, M. and Stroebe, W. (1987). Productivity loss in brainstorming groups: Toward the solution of a riddle. *Journal of Personality and Social Psychology* 53(3).

Dutton, J.E. (2003). *Energize Your Workplace: How to Create and Sustain High-Quality Connections at Work*. Jossey-Bass.

Dweck, C. (2007). *Mindset: The New Psychology of Success*. Random House.

Dweck, C. (2010). How can you change from a fixed mindset to a growth mindset? http://mindsetonline.com/changeyourmindset/firststeps/index.html (accessed 9 December 2016).

Edmondson, A. (1999). Psychological safety and learning behavior in work teams. *Administrative Science Quarterly* 44 (2).

Fisher, R. and Ury, W. (1981). *Getting to Yes: Negotiating Agreement Without Giving In*. Penguin Books.

Fredrickson, B. (2001). The role of positive emotions in positive psychology: The broaden-and-build theory of positive emotions. *American Psychologist* 56(3).

Garfinkle, J.A. (2011). *Getting Ahead: Three Steps to Take Your Career to the Next Level*. John Wiley & Sons.

Gibbs, G. (1988). *Learning by Doing*. Oxford Brookes University.

Goffee, R. and Jones, G. (2006). Why should anyone be led by you? *Harvard Business Review*, September–October 2006.

Goldberg, L.R. (1992). The development of markers for the big-five factor structure. *Psychological Assessment* 4(1).

Goleman, D. (1995). *Emotional Intelligence: Why It Can Matter More Than IQ for Character, Health and Lifelong Achievement*. Bantam Books.

Goltz, S. (2014). A closer look at personas: A guide to developing the right ones. https://www.smashingmagazine.com/2014/08/a-closer-look-at-personas-part-2/ (accessed 30 July 2017).

Gouillart, F. and Sturdivant, F. (1994). Spend a day in the life of your customers. *Harvard Business Review*, January–February, 1994.

Greenberger, D. and Padesky, C.A. (2016). *Mind Over Mood* (2nd ed.). Guilford Press.

Gremler, D.D. and Gwinner, K.P. (2008). Rapport-building behaviors used by retail employees. *Journal of Retailing* 84(3).

Grove, A.S. (1995). *High-Output Management*. Random House.

Gruwez, E. (2014). *Presentation Thinking and Design: Create Better Presentations, Quicker*. Pearson UK.

Hansen, M.T. and Birkinshaw, J. (2007.). The innovation value chain. *Harvard Business Review*, June 2007.

Harding, S. and Long, T. (1998). *Proven Management Models*. Gower Publishing.

Harter, J.K., Schmidt, F.L., and Keyes, C.L.M. (2002).Well-being in the workplace and its relationship to business outcomes: A review of the Gallup studies. http://media.gallup.com/documents/whitePaper—Well-BeingInTheWorkplace.pdf (accessed 18 June 2017).

Hassani B. (2016). *Scenario Analysis in Risk Management: Theory and Practice in Finance*. Springer.

Heath, C. and Heath, D. (2007). *Made to Stick: Why Some Ideas Survive and Others Die*. Random House.

Heintzman, M., Leathers, D.G., Parrott, R.L. et al. (1993). Nonverbal rapport-building behaviors' effects on perceptions of a supervisor. *Management Communication Quarterly* 7(2).

Heron, J. (2001). *Helping the Client: A Creative, Practical Guide*. Sage.

Herzberg, F. (1968). One more time: How do you motivate employees? *Harvard Business Review*, January–February, 1968.

Heyd, D. (2008). Tact: Sense, sensitivity, and virtue. *Inquiry: An Interdisciplinary Journal of Philosophy* 38(3).

Hill, T. and Westbrook, R. (1997). SWOT analysis: It's time for a product recall. *Long Range Planning* 30(1).

Hofstede, G., Hofstede, G.J., and Minkov, M. (2010). *Cultures and Organizations, Software of the Mind*. McGraw-Hill.

Hogan, R. and Kaiser, R.B. (2005). What we know about leadership. *Review of General Psychology* 9(2).

Ibarra, H. (2003). *Working Identity: Unconventional Strategies for Reinventing Your Career*. Harvard Business Review Press.

Judge, T.A., Klinger, R.L., Rodell, J.B. et al. (2013). Hierarchical representations of the five-factor model of personality in predicting job performance. *Journal of Applied Psychology* 98(6).

Judge, T.A., Locke, E.A., Durham, C.C. et al. (1998). Dispositional effects on job and life satisfaction: The role of core evaluations. *Journal of Applied Psychology* 83(1).

Kahneman, D. (2012). *Thinking Fast and Slow*. Penguin.

Kahneman, D., Lovallo, D., and Sibony, O. (2011). The big idea: Before you make that big decision … *Harvard Business Review,* June 2011.

Keeley, L., Walters, H., Pikkel, R. et al. (2013). *Ten Types of Innovation: The Discipline of Building Breakthroughs*. John Wiley &Sons.

Kenett, R.S. (2008). Cause-and-effect diagrams. In: *Encyclopedia of Statistics in Quality and Reliability*. John Wiley & Sons.

Kern, M., Waters, L., Adler, A. et al. (2014). Assessing employee wellbeing in schools using a multifaceted approach. *Psychology* 5:500–513.

Kessler, E.H. (2013). The appreciative inquiry model. In: *Encyclopedia of Management Theory*. Sage Publications.

Kim-Keung Ho, J. (2014). Formulation of a systemic PEST analysis for strategic analysis. *European Academic Research* 2(5).

King, V. (2016). *The 10 keys to happier living*. Headline Publishing Group, London.

Klingsieck, K.B. (2013). When good things don't come to those who wait. *European Psychologist* 18(1):24–34.

Kohn, W. and Smith, M. (2011). Collaborative fixation: Effects of others' ideas on brainstorming. *Applied Cognitive Psychology* 25(3).

Kolko, J. (2015). Design thinking comes of age. *Harvard Business Review*, September 2015.

Kotter, J.P. (1995). Leading change: Why transformation efforts fail. *Harvard Business Review*, March–April 1995.

Kübler-Ross, E. (1969). *On Death and Dying*. Macmillan.

Lamm, H. and Trommsdorff, G. (1973). Group versus individual performance on tasks requiring ideational proficiency (brainstorming): A review. *European Journal of Social Psychology* 3(4).

Lencioni, P.M. (2005). *Overcoming the Five Dysfunctions of a Team: A Field Guide for Leaders, Managers and Facilitators*. Jossey-Bass.

Lewicki, R.J. and Hiam, A. (2010). *Mastering Business Negotiation: A Working Guide to Making Deals and Resolving Conflict*. Jossey-Bass.

Locke, E.A. and Latham, G.P. (2013). *New Developments in Goal Setting and Task Performance*. Routledge.

Locke, E.A. and Latham, G.P. (2016). New directions in goal setting theory. *Current Directions in Psychological Science* 15(5).

Loo, R. (2002). Journaling: A learning tool for project management training and team-building. *The Project Management Institute* 33(4).

Luft, J. (1982). The Johari window: A graphic model of awareness in interpersonal relations. In: *ITL Reading Book for Human Relations Training*. NTL Institute.

Lyons, S. and Kuron, L. (2014). Generational differences in the workplace: A review of the evidence and directions for future research. *Journal of Organizational Behavior* 35.

Manktelow, J. (2015). ORAPAPA: A checklist for making better decisions. https://www.mindtools.com/pages/article/orapapa.htm (accessed 11 December 2016).

Manktelow, J. (2015). Team-specific motivation. https://www.mindtools.com/pages/article/team-specific-motivation.htm (accessed 9 August 2017).

Martin, P.D. and Pope, J. (2008). Competency-based interviewing—Has it gone too far? *Industrial and Commercial Training* 40(2).

Mathieu, J.E. and Rapp, T.L. (2009). Laying the foundation for successful team performance trajectories: The roles of team charters and performance strategies. *Journal of Applied Psychology* 94(1).

Meharabian, A. (1971). *Silent Messages*. Wadsworth Publishing Company.

Mencl, J. and Lester, S.W. (2014). More alike than different. *Journal of Leadership and Organizational Studies* 21(3).

Mendelow, A.L. (1981). Environmental scanning—The impact of the stakeholder concept. ICIS 1981 proceedings.

Miller, P. and Wedell-Wedellsborg, T. (2013). The case for stealth innovation. *Harvard Business Review*, March 2013.

Misner, I. (2010). *Networking Like a Pro: Turning Contacts Into Connections*. Entrepreneur Press.

Moll, J. et al. (2006). Human fronto-mesolimbic networks guide decisions about charitable donation. *Proceedings of the National Academy of Sciences of the USA* 103(42).

Nay, R. (2014). *The Anger Management Workbook*. Guilford Press.

Osterwalder, A. and Pigneur, Y. (2010). *Business Model Generation*. Wiley.

Parker, S.K. and Axtell, C.M. (2001). Seeing another viewpoint: Antecedents and outcomes of employee perspective taking. *Academy of Management Journal* 44(6).

Paulus, P.B. and Brown, V.R. (2007). Toward more creative and innovative group idea generation: A cognitive-social-motivational perspective of brainstorming. *Social and Personality Psychology Compass* 1(1).

Prahalad, C.K. and Hamel, G. (1990). The core competence of the corporation. *Harvard Business Review*, May–June 1990.

Prince-Embury, S. (2013). Translating resilience theory for assessment and application with children, adolescents and adults. In: *Resilience in Children, Adolescents and Adults* (eds., S. Prince-Embury and D.H. Saklofske). Springer.

Project Management Institute. (2017). *A Guide to the Project Management Body of Knowledge (PMBOK Guide)* (6th ed.). Philadelphia.

Rawson, A., Duncan, E., and Jones, C. (2013). The truth about customer experience. *Harvard Business Review*, September 2013.

Risdon, C. (2015). 10 most interesting examples of customer journey maps. http://blog.uxeria.com/en/10-most-interesting-examples-of-customer-journey-maps/ (accessed 30 July 2017).

Robison, J. (2006). In praise of praising your employees. *Gallup Business Journal.* http://news.gallup.com/businessjournal/25369/praise-praising-your-employees.aspx (accessed 31 December 2017).

Rooney, J.J. and Vanden Heuvel, L.N. (2004). Root cause analysis for beginners. *Quality Progress.* https://servicelink.pinnacol.com/pinnacol_docs/lp/cdrom_web/safety/management/accident_investigation/Root_Cause.pdf (accessed 31 December 2017).

Rosenthal, T.L. and Zimmerman, B.J. (1978). *Social Learning and Cognition.* Academic Press.

Rothblum, E.D. (1990). Fear of failure: The psychodynamic, need achievement, fear of success, and procrastination models. In: *Handbook of Social and Evaluation Anxiety* (ed. H. Leitenberg). Springer.

Rozovsky, J. (2015). The five keys to a successful Google team. https://rework.withgoogle.com/blog/five-keys-to-a-successful-google-team (accessed 4 August 2017).

Rubin, R. (2002). Will the real SMART goals please stand up? http://www.siop.org/tip/backissues/tipapr02/03rubin.aspx (accessed 11 December 2016).

Rummler, G.A. and Brache. A.P. (1995). *Improving Performance: How to Manage the White Space on the Organization Chart.* John Wiley & Sons.

Saxena, P. (2015). Johari window: An effective model for improving interpersonal communication and managerial effectiveness. *SIT Journal of Management* 5(2).

Scott, C., Dunn, A.M., Williams, E.B. et al. (2015). Implementing after-action review systems in organizations—Key principles and practical considerations. In: *The Cambridge Handbook of Meeting Science.* Cambridge University Press.

Schaupp, M. (2017). Why a management concept fails to support managers' work: The case of the "core competence of a corporation." *Management Learning* 48(1).

Schlack, J.W. (2015). Use your customers as ethnographers. *Harvard Business Review*, August 2015.

Schwartz, P. (1991). *Art of the Long View*. Profile Books.

Seligman, M.E.P. (2011). *Flourish: A Visionary New Understanding of Happiness and Well-being*. Free Press.

Slovic, P., Finucane, M.L., Peters, E. et al. Risk as analysis and risk as feelings: Some thoughts about affect, reason, risk and rationality. *Risk Analysis* 24.

Society for Human Resource Management. (2015). How to develop a job description. https://www.shrm.org/resourcesandtools/tools-and-samples/how-to-guides/pages/developajobdescription.aspx (accessed 4 August 2017).

Sommer, S., Bendoly, E., and Kavadias, S. (2015). *Search strategies in complex and ambiguous problem spaces*. Working paper.

Stajkovic, A.D. and Luthans, F. (2002). Social cognitive theory and self-efficacy: Implications for motivation theory and practice. In: *Motivation and Work Behavior* (eds. L. Porter, G. Bigley, and R.M. Steers). McGraw-Hill/Irwin.

Stallworth Williams, L. (2008). The mission statement: A corporate reporting tool with a past, present, and future. *Linda North Georgia College and State University Journal of Business Communication* 45(2).

Tamir, D. and Mitchell, J. (2012). Disclosing information about the self is intrinsically rewarding. *Proceedings of the National Academy of Sciences* 109(21).

Tedeshi, R.G. and Calhoun, L.G. (2004). *Posttraumatic Growth: Conceptual Foundation and Empirical Evidence*. Lawrence Erlbaum Associates.

Tickle-Degnen, L. and Rosenthal, R. (1990). The nature of rapport and its nonverbal correlates. *Psychological Inquiry* 1(4).

Tims, M. and Bakker, A.B. (2010). Job crafting: Towards a new model of individual job redesign. *SA Journal of Industrial Psychology* 36(2).

Ullrich, P. and Lutgendorf, S. (2002). Journal about stressful events: Effects of cognitive processing and emotional expression. *Annals of Behavioral Medicine* 24(3).

Van Eck, M. and van Zanten, E. (2014). *The One Page Business Strategy*. FT Publishing International.

Vigoda-Gadot, E. and Dryzin-Amit, Y. (2006). Organizational politics, leadership and performance in modern public worksites: A theoretical framework. In: *Handbook of Organizational Politics* (eds. E. Vigoda-Gadot and Y. Dryzin-Amit). Edward Elgar Publishing.

Walker, D.H.T., Bourne, L.M., and Shelley, A. (2008). Influence, stakeholder mapping and visualization. *Journal of Construction Management and Economics* 26(6).

Weydt, A. (2010). Developing delegation skills. *The Online Journal of Issues in Nursing* 15(2).

Whetten, D.A. and Cameron, K.S. (2010). *Developing Management Skills* (8th ed.). Pearson Education, Inc.

Williams, J. (2009). *Coaching for Performance* (4th ed.). Nicholas Brealey Publishing.

Wójcicka, D. (2011). The anatomy of an experience map. http://adaptivepath.org/ideas/the-anatomy-of-an-experience-map/ (accessed 30 July 2017).

Woolley, A.W., Chabris, C.F., Pentland, A. et al. (2010). Evidence for a collective intelligence factor in the performance of human groups. *Science* 330(6004).

Wrzesniewski, A. and Dutton, J.E. (2001). Crafting a job: Revisioning employees as active crafters of their work. *Academy of Management Review* 2.

Yukl, G. (2012). *Leadership in Organizations* (8th ed.). Pearson Education.

Zack, D. (2010). *Networking for People Who Hate Networking: A Field Guide for Introverts, the Overwhelmed, and the Underconnected*. Berrett-Koehler Publishers.

Zuckerman, M., Kuhlman, D.M., Joireman, J. et al. (1993). A comparison of three structural models for personality: The big three, the big five, and the alternative five. *Journal of Personality and Social Psychology* 65(4).

Index

Page references followed by *fig* indicate an illustrated figure.